focus
practice
empower
HOPE

KINDLING HOPE

Kindling Hope

DAILY PASSAGES FROM DARKNESS INTO LIGHT

ZHEN-RU

Translated by Amrita Translation Foundation
in collaboration with Kacy Lin

POWNAL STREET PRESS
CHARLOTTETOWN

www.kindling-hope.com

Pownal Street Press · www.pownalstreetpress.com

Cataloging data available from Library and Archives Canada ISBN 9-781-998129-29-4 · eBook ISBN: 9-781-998129-35-5

Edited by Maureen Duffy and Emma Campanero · Copy edited by Alison Strumberger · Typeset by Jordan Beaulieu · Artwork by Clara Encinas

Pownal Street Press gratefully acknowledges Mi'kma'ki, the ancestral and unceded territory of the Mi'kmaq First Nation on whose land our office is located.

Printed and bound in Canada by Friesens.

2 3 4 5 6 25 26 27 28 29

Table of Contents

To my beloved teachers,
my dearest mother and father,
and every person searching for their path.

Foreword

Kacy Lin

In the auditorium at the University of Prince Edward Island, hundreds of people gather to listen to a lecture by Zhen-Ru. Full of anticipation and excitement, we rise as she walks toward the podium, hands joined in prayer. Wearing a dark blue dress, her dark hair flows past her waist. She reaches the podium and together we bow to the Buddha.

Today is a day many of her students have dreamed of. Students come to Prince Edward Island from all over the world to join her, including Los Angeles, New York, Shanghai, Singapore, Sydney, Taipei, Toronto, and Vancouver.

She begins, "Today, we will be discussing the *150 Verses* by Aśvaghoṣa. But first, let me share how we came to this translation." Much to my surprise, she begins by explaining the origins of the translations—from Sanskrit, to Tibetan, and finally to Chinese.

The ticking of the auditorium clock sounds louder and louder. Having expected something less academic, I find my thoughts wandering.

As she is describing its origins, I continuously wonder: *Why not move to the meaningful parts of Aśvaghoṣa's verses?* This lecture feels tedious, full of specific terminology relating to the Tibetan language. Still, Zhen-Ru repeatedly engages the crowd, telling jokes, anecdotes, and stories to get us through the history of the *150 Verses.*

During the lecture, I cannot help but wonder:
Why do I need this tedious introduction?

Later, when I have an opportunity to consult with one of her students, he mentions, "After the lecture, I spoke with Teacher Zhen-Ru. I said, 'Teacher, I feel like it was really brave of you to share that lecture.' She replied, 'I am not brave. I felt in my marrow that its origins were meaningful. So, I had to go on.'"

I thought silently to myself: *Oftentimes, things that have come into fruition are taken for granted. As with this lecture on the history of the* 150 Verses, *how often do I trace the things I use to their origins?*

The words I have written on this page,
the images they conjure,
the sounds they make as they land in my mind,
the understandings they give rise to—

how many people have gifted me
with words, language, and connection?

And to them,
am I grateful?

As in Zhen-Ru's poem "The Giving Tree" (p. 249):

Standing before an ancient tree,
we may marvel at how lush its leaves are and
how sturdy its trunk is,
and some,
with a heart of gratitude will ponder:

Years ago,
who planted this tree,
so that today
I have this shade?

In this moment, I felt this passage applying to more than the trees. Perhaps the hard work and compassion of others are hidden in all things.

Translator's Note

Amrita Translation Foundation

The idea of compiling passages for daily use germinated in 2017. Over the past decade, the world we have known has greatly increased in complexity. Former black swan events are now regular occurrences. Natural disasters, wars, and economic stresses are a mainstay in our newsfeeds. Layered on top of existing interpersonal issues, we are all balancing on a tightrope, ready to topple over at the slightest push, with no safety net in sight.

As a Buddhist practitioner and spiritual teacher for over two decades, Zhen-Ru has met with people from all walks of life and shared her understanding of Buddhist teachings with them. Her teachings range from the extremely profound Buddhist discourse to applying Buddhist principles in seemingly simple everyday occurrences. As her students, we've personally experienced the way her teachings offer us a simple shift in perspective—backed by logic—bringing us from darkness to light.

And so, the thought of putting together a book with passages from Zhen-Ru's teachings took hold.

We chose passages that have helped us greatly in our everyday challenges. Be it difficult interpersonal relationships, overcoming defeats, or dealing with hurt, we hope there is something for everyone.

This book can serve the reader however feels right in the moment. You can sit down and read it from cover to cover, slowly taking in the variety of themes. Or you can flip to a random page and get a quick spoonful of wisdom. Or perhaps diving into a certain theme can help you in your current challenge.

Regardless of how the book is read, we've found the passages are most effective when we savour each word and contemplate their meaning, reflecting on how each relates to our own day-to-day lives and experiences. Allow every word to be a window to peer into and discover another fresh, boundless world. Our personal experience has been that reading a passage repeatedly, and often recalling it as we go about our day, helps us remember the words in times of difficulty. And of course, discussions with friends, exploring each word, is extremely enriching, as we discover new facets and deepen our understanding.

As you read the passages, you may find yourself a bit perplexed at times. Valuing efficiency, we're eager to get into the "how" of things. If changes need to be made, let them be made! The faster the better. But we tend to overlook the nuances of how our mind works, stalling the process instead. When we resonate with a concept, we immediately want to put it into practice. But we often adopt a new practice, only to be disappointed when we drop it a few days later.

New habits take time; they also need to be fully embraced. Sometimes a theory is good only in theory. Our minds aren't *ready* to adopt it yet; there are too many resisting thoughts. So before jumping into "how," we need to first pause and ask ourselves: do I truly believe this will be good for me? And we need to dig deep. Many of Zhen-Ru's passages seem to stop before giving us the "how." This is intentional. The break allows us a chance to examine whether we truly agree with what's being said.

Zhen-Ru's wish to accompany all readers through difficult times led to this English edition of *Kindling Hope*. It is truly a labour of love, an arduous six-year-long effort. Many of the passages were extracted from teachings to an audience with a Buddhist background. The hardest issue we faced was finding the English vocabulary that could bridge the gap between easy understanding and staying true to the Buddhist concepts. Commonly used English words typically have pre-existing connotations. Esoteric words—no one would understand what the passage was about.

Though we have done our best to capture the essence of Zhen-Ru's teachings in our English translation, within each language system, there will always be some context that cannot be completely transferred over. As such, we thought we could leave a note here about a few words that we've used repeatedly to provide more context to the reader. For instance, the word "good" is used several times to translate the Chinese word *shan* (善), sometimes interchangeably with the words "kind" or "virtuous." Within a Buddhist context, "good" is not specific to a subjective affinity, but rather, actions of the body, speech, and mind that result in happiness free from afflictions and their side-effects.

"Suffering" is not restricted to our mental or physical ailments but contains a broader meaning. In Buddhism, suffering in saṃsāra (the cycle of life, death, and rebirth) is a constant undercurrent we're not necessarily aware of. In addition to obvious discomforts and distress, suffering exists because we typically don't see things as they are. There is not one thing in saṃsāra we can continually experience without eventually feeling inklings of displeasure.

Far from a fatalistic approach to life, the Buddhist mentality is one of empowerment. We form the bonds of saṃsāra, but we are also the ones who can break them by battling our afflictions, the real culprit of our suffering. "Afflictions" are the destructive emotions that disrupt clarity and peace of mind. Every affliction has its antidote. Every battle is an opportunity to grow.

As in the Four Noble Truths, Buddhists believe that by recognizing the suffering and the causes of suffering, we can take the path of inner cultivation, ultimately transcending our suffering and finding enlightenment. The power is in our hands. As Zhen-Ru so deftly articulates, we are our own protagonist, director, and script writer.

We hope respite can be found within these passages, and the words can journey with the reader to uncover their inner strength and hope. As Zhen-Ru's students, we are humbled to have been part of the translation process. We hope you will find the passages as helpful as we've found them in our life's journey.

Opening Poem

Perhaps you may not recognize me
but that does not much matter.

The winds continue to blow,
the clouds continue to drift,
the scents of flowers continue to waft.
We are together,
bathed in the universe,
immersed in life's glory.

Somewhere, by lamplight,
I am composing my poem.
Somewhere, beneath the eaves,
you are singing a song you love.

Within the poem and the song
lingers the richness of life,
sweet, like the fruit-laden branches of summer.

We ardently love life
and the world in which we live.

The moon climbs in the sky,
full, vast, and round,
bearing the gazes of people through history
and their yearnings for reunion after separation.
Now we gaze upon the moon, you and I!

Anticipating,
the day every living being
has a heart as luminous as the moon,
a mind never unsettled,
eternally free from distress,
in boundless serenity!

The stars come out of hiding
as the frogs sing in harmony.
The child, holding father's hand while walking,
has questions outnumbering the stars.

Oh, children!
Children as beautiful and pure as the stars.
Are they not what all humans hold dear?
For them to have
clean mountains, clear water, and crisp air,
we will make every effort,
endeavouring to change all that is imperfect.

Child, do you know?
Have Mama's and Papa's hair
already turned pale as snow?
It is time that has stolen its richness.
Meanwhile,
we have miraculously grown strong and beautiful.

Mother and Father!
In the snows of winter
our youth is the glowing fire in the hearth,
warming and illuminating your lives.

We earnestly light gratitude's kindling,
when the cotton-white snowflakes kiss the ground,
like a flame that cannot be contained,
these words swell within me:
Mother, Father, my love for you knows no bounds.

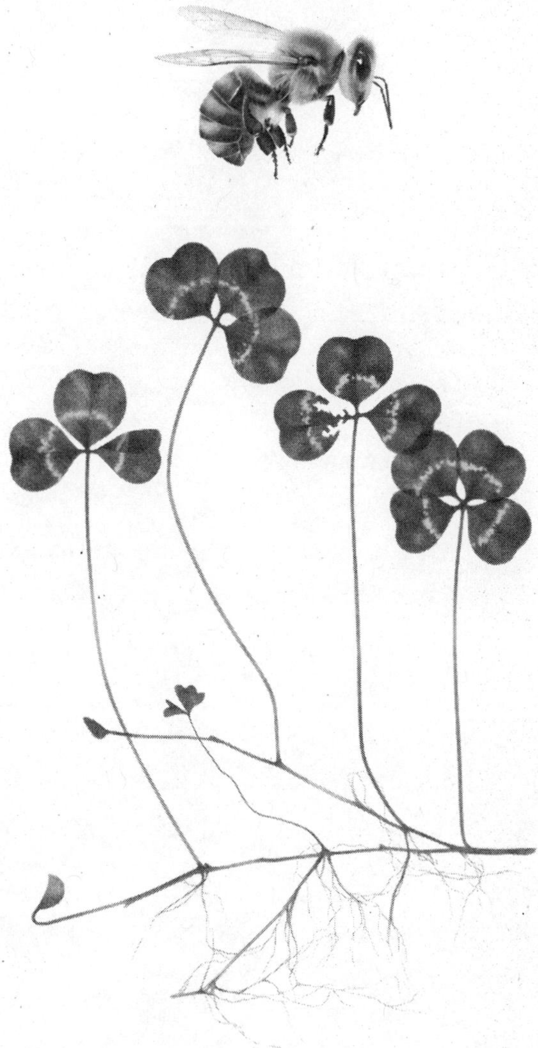

CHAPTER ONE

Seeds of the Rising Sun

Daybreak

Daybreak, the sky is crystal clear.
Behind towering mountains,
the morning rays are radiant.
Surging forth, their flares engrave the sky.
Illuminating and emanating great power,
the source from which all things grow and flourish—
this is the nature of good deeds.

The Morning Light

When we begin
let us commence with a lustrous aspiration—
like the rising sun at the start of a new day—
allowing our tasks to begin with brightness.

Like a surrounding of trees
quietly bringing out the hues of red flowers,
in our daily life,
there are those who work alongside us.
Let us not forget them!
Many accomplishments depend on teamwork.

So when attending to tasks,
we keep true to a kind heart toward others,
like a flower blooming in the morning light
holding a delightful fragrance within
and being an idyllic scene for others.

Planting Seeds

The law of cause and effect can be obscure—
difficult to discover and understand.

The acorn, though tiny,
has the potential to become a giant oak
whose wood can be used for many things:
hardwood floors, wooden panels,
house frames and more—
the possibilities are limitless.

Similarly our karma also grows and expands—
a small seed can develop into a great fruit.
When you give to others
you sow a tiny seed of generosity.
As you continuously nurture this seed
with joy and sincerity,
it expands—exponentially!

Darkness and Light

Consider—
a group gathers,
they analyze how to destroy others.
From dawn to dusk
their thoughts revolve around how to
ruin others' reputations, friends, and families,
contemplating how to
threaten all that is beautiful in their lives.
In the process of hurting others, their thoughts relish.

Consider—
another group gathers,
they explore how to help others.
From dawn to dusk
their thoughts revolve around how to
support others,
helping their reputations rise, and
their relationships with friends and family flourish—
contemplating how to
give others all that is wonderful within the world,
thinking of how to
make this beauty sustainable and ever-increasing.
In the process of helping others, their thoughts relish.

These two groups of people are like
darkness and light.
Which would you want to be with?

Make Great Aspirations

The greatness of our aspirations
and the greatness of our kind intentions
determine how greatly we impact the world.
When making wishes, never hold back.
Those who are too afraid to make great aspirations
will suffer great losses—
the power of the mind is boundless.
The more we limit our minds,
the more ensnared we will be.
The more ensnared we are,
the more unhappiness we feel.
We confine ourselves to prisons of our own making.

Untying Tethers

Encircling hurt
continuously walking—
a thousand rounds—
still stagnant.

Can we
cast away
old habits and
leave our tether behind?
In life,
can we
run
toward
joy?

Escaping from Negative Thoughts

Suffering is a soft chain
enveloping us when we are not
aware.
Before we know it, we are
ensnared
negativity suffocating our thoughts
like pain spreading throughout.

We must
break free from suffering's grasp
burst through negativity's cocoon.
We must
give rise to positive thoughts—
even a thought as delicate as a strand of hair
as small as a grain of sand is
precious—
why?
As long as it rises
hope rises.

The Most Extraordinary Thing

To lead a meaningful life
we do not have to do extraordinary things
for the most extraordinary thing is our heart.

Perhaps we are only
sweeping the floor or cleaning the table
but once we have a meaningful goal
bringing together all of our
thoughts, words, and actions,
we will lead an extraordinary life.

One day
we will feel our heart shining like the sun,
illuminating the world.
This is the brightness of our inner nature.
This is its extraordinary bloom.

Sowing the Seeds of Nobility

Why practice humility,
treating everyone with respect
as if they were one's honoured guests?

When one is of service to others,
one sows the seeds of nobility!

The ability to serve others
through our actions, words, and thoughts,
assisting them and gifting their lives
with sprinklings of joy
is truly a unique characteristic
of being human.

Regaining Vibrancy

When someone has done us wrong
yet we still choose to be with them,
we continue to fulfill life's responsibilities.
We endure the pressure from the wrongdoing.
It's been rough.

Is it possible for us to stop reliving
the wrong the other has inflicted?
Every reliving is toxic—
this rumination only etches the anguish more deeply.

Why not use a fresh mindset to face what's ahead?
In every opportunity—
proactively—
create novel virtuous karma.
Let our lives regain the vibrancy to create.
Swiftly heal our wounds.
Stride on!
We can do it!

Clearing the Heart's Haze

Anxious and depressed feelings
are haze within the heart.
Negative thoughts are the polluted air
they arise from.

What if we start thinking positively?
Look!
Within life,
how much marvel is unseen?
How many kind acts are forgotten?
Find things that give rise to gratitude and happiness—
placing them within the heart,
thinking on them often,
perhaps writing ten a day,
can gradually clear the air within.

The Gardener

When we hope to assist others,
when our hearts are sincere
in our wish to support them,
we are like gardeners—
step, sow
sow, step.
As we are sowing seeds,
despite the appearance of only soil beneath trees,
come spring—
walking and watching,
you will find
they have become a meadow of flowers,
blooming as far as the eye can see.

A Grander Terrain

Once our propensity to care for others
grows more magnanimous,
we sense the heart
becoming as vast as the ocean and
as limitless as the sky.

Exploring a grander terrain,
shall we give it a try?

Instinct Comes with Practice

If we do acts of kindness
and are attentive of others when possible,
this will become a habit with time.
Eventually—
with little effort—
we will instinctively understand what others need.

At the Source

Happiness grows on a bed of kindness
of your own making.
It flourishes not from the attention of others and
not from the comforts they offer—
your own kind thoughts
are the grounds upon which joy arises
and the foundation from where it begins.

The Blessed

Becoming numb to things others have done—
does this mean the heart has become frigid?
A cold—indifferent—heart,
is it a joyful one?
No.
Never.

A heart full of gratitude
is the happiest one.

Autumn's Grace

Gazing afar—
autumn's fields
colours abound
a joyous harvest!

Oh, teachers!
Within my heart's open meadows
are bountiful kind acts
bestowed by your compassion.
My heart is full and thankful.

Effervescing with Joy

Searching for things that inspire elation
allows us to effervesce with great joy each day.

Discover others' kindness,
discover your own—
doing so will bring wondrous joy!

The Roots of Light

In the darkness, lost amidst the choices before us
it is only with the light that
our teachers have kindled in our heart that
the path beneath our feet is illuminated.

When we are tormented and on the precipice
it is only through remembering
the words of our teachers
and remembering their loving kindness,
that we find the strength to declare,

I will not give up.

Cultivate Optimism

Always consider
how can I be proactive?
Spare no effort
in training yourself to see
the positive and joyful aspects of every situation.

Once you master this
no matter what challenges arise
you will be brave and full of positivity as
your eyes focus on the blessings.
Everything you see
will begin to bloom with infinite potential.

Your path is bright.
Your joy is boundless.

Bidding Farewell to Regret

Rather than complaining about—
and feeling regretful for—
everything that is imperfect in our lives,
why not sow seeds
and grow what we are missing?
Then—
in the future—
our lives will be full of abundance!

Emotional Storage

Sadness, sadness, and more sadness
will accumulate.
Fury, fury, and more fury
will accumulate.
Happiness, happiness, and more happiness
will also accumulate.
What do you truly want to store
in your emotional warehouse?

Sparks of Benevolence

One positive act lights a beacon.
When the beacon begins to shine,
then slowly, others will also begin to burn.
The world becomes brighter and brighter,
dispelling the darkness.

What is the spark that lights these beacons?
Your benevolence, the spark.

Your care, the fuel.

Happiness in Tow

When we realize we have habitual thought patterns
that cause great bitterness in our lives
we must find ways to replace them with
joyous thought patterns.

With joyous thought patterns,
we have a joyous mindset
and in turn, a joyous life.
If we are joyous, we spread joy
to our family and to our friends.

No matter where we go
we bring happiness in tow.
Joy is truly a precious gift—
a person with joy lives in great abundance.

Holding on to Our Goals

Sometimes when we're low in spirits,
we may consider abandoning our goals.
However, when we really think about it,
these feelings give us an even more
powerful reason to persist.

Feeling sullen is from negative karmic seeds
planted in the past.

If we can use
all the opportunities we have
to engage in spiritual practice
and sow positive karmic seeds,
we will be uplifted in the future!

Not So Small Steps

We may believe that in life
every step toward virtue
every step in transcending our limits
is smaller than a grain of sand.
But in truth,
the power and effect
from these tiny steps
may be larger than the universe.

Hold Fast to Hope

Everyone has potential—
because of impermanence
everyone can change.
If we do not lose sight of hope
there is endless hope for our next generations.
With time, wisdom, and boundless compassion,
everything is possible.

Walking in the Dawn

Happiness is a practice.
When we are walking in the dawn
when we catch sight of a leaf wearing dewdrops
when we see a bird singing heartily on a branch
when we see the faces of people rushing by—
can we gift a delightful smile and
share a beautiful blessing?

Two Thoughts Encounter an Obstacle

When encountering an obstacle, we can think
This problem has me cornered
and because of this,
feel anxious and down.
Or we can think
I'm ready to overcome this problem, because
it only shows where I can improve and grow wiser!
Therefore,
we can proactively search for ways to overcome it.

The latter is exciting
with a hint of anticipation
and a feeling of infinite hope.

Planting Even More Joy

There is joy and serenity when
our inner realizations spark.
But the joy of seeing the seeds
we have laboriously sown in others—
sprouting, growing, and
gently swaying beneath the sunlight—
this is an even greater joy!

More exhilarating than soaring in the clouds,
more fervent than the ocean's endless waves,
more breathtaking than the earth's most vivid views.

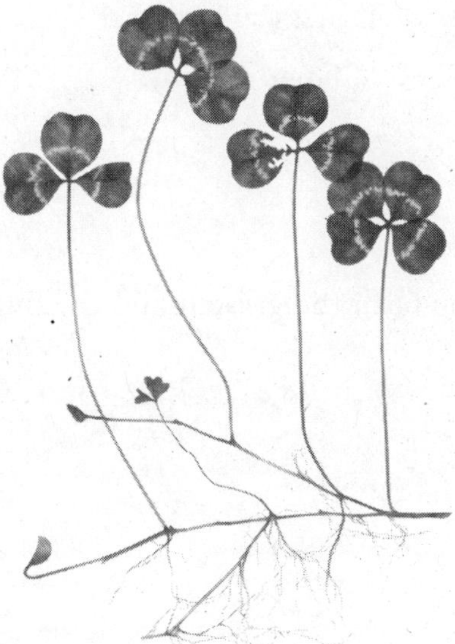

Humanity's Greatest Strength

Transforming a negative situation
into a positive one is not an easy process,
but it can be done with determination and
a proper approach.

What is humanity's greatest strength?

The power of the mind.

How do we obtain such a power?

Through proactive thinking.
The moment we harness such power
we will be able to change destiny.

What is changing destiny?

It is changing both the present and the future.

The Script of Life

Life—
moment by moment,
it continuously flows forward.
And the future?
It's tightly intertwined with
what we're doing in the present.
We're writing our script,
we're the director
and eventually
we're the star.
When writing the script of our future,
let's not write ourselves into a tragedy—
instead,
we'll write ourselves to be
happy and joyful,
prosperous,
dignified,
smart,
full of innate good.

Happiness is a Skill

Noticing happiness
is a skill we can develop—
refining our sensitivity to joy
let's not be numb.
This ability is incredibly valuable,
more valuable than wealth.
And the best thing?
Feeling joy is nourished through practice!

Gripping Negative Feelings by the Scruff of Their Neck

How do we put a stop to negative feelings?
We must give rise to their antidote.
Where do these negative feelings start?
In our thoughts.

Controlling our thoughts,
we can hold these negative feelings by the scruff of their neck, and stop our lives from descending into the most painful places.

Looking Within for a Way Out

When we look for the causes of suffering within
we give ourselves a way out.

This is something we have control over,
something we can eliminate.

If the causes of suffering are within another person
our hands are tied.
Precisely because the causes of suffering are within me,
as soon as I learn the methods to wipe it out,
I can thoroughly eliminate it!

This is what we mean by
looking within.

Happiness: Within Heart's Reach

The moment we see that
the root of all problems lies within
will we not feel inspired and happy?

If it were hidden in the ocean
it would be a problem!
The ocean is so large
it would be difficult to find.

If it is in the heart,
if I resolve to find it,
I will locate the source of my problems and
eliminate it—
it's even easier than riding a bike,
costs almost nothing,
and can bring more happiness than
anything else in the world.

Engaging in Kindness

If we choose
to focus on how awful others are all day
and how we did nothing wrong,
does this help us engage in kindness?

Or
would the world feel like an unpleasant place,
as we live our day in low spirits?

Rather,
Observing Merits and Appreciating Kindness
allows us to see
others' contributions
others' kind thoughts
and
all the inherent goodness hiding within
others' hearts.

A Small Positive Seed

Just like how a tiny seed can grow into a giant tree,
great effects can rise from small actions.

This magnification of karma can be intimidating,
especially when we realize that
doing a small non-virtuous deed—
without repentance—
can magnify into something terrible.

However, there's an uplifting side to the same coin.
When we do a small virtuous deed—
as long as we don't regret it or destroy it with anger—
it will grow into unimaginable joy!

Self-Victory

When facing challenges,
if we continuously surrender, we may eventually
develop the habit of withdrawing.
In time, we lose the courage to face anything.
We may miss out on the greatest benefit and
become powerless to find true happiness
for ourselves and others.

However,
if we take such habits—
feeling incapable, inert, or rationalizing—
step atop them and move forward,
we can transcend ourselves!
Our lives will be full of the sweet taste of self-victory!
Like a champion standing upon a mountaintop,
gazing at the world—
it is vast and ours to behold.

Changing the World from Within

When we give rise to a compassionate thought,
when we have a curious inkling for
the wisdom of emptiness—
in these moments, we change the world.

As we transform our minds,
the people around us naturally benefit.
We leave tragedy one step further behind, and
take one step toward a world that is more beautiful.

As We Sow, So We Reap

Karma is like throwing rice in the air—
in the end, it lands on ourselves.
Speaking ill of others is like spitting in the air
or raising a fiery torch against the wind—
in the end, it all lands on ourselves.

Filling our Baskets

Our day is
an empty basket.
We must carefully select what we place inside.
If we place an assortment of fresh flowers,
then we carry a basket
of gentle sweetness.

Seeing Our Worth

As we help one another
we see our worth reflected in other people's lives.
This sense of worth can
turn us away from a road to ruin
because as soon as we realize
I am worthwhile
we will not choose to destroy ourselves—
we will choose to love ourselves.

The Fortitude of an Oak Tree

A small seed
has unimaginable strength.
It transcends winter
conserving energy in the barren cold.
With spring's arrival
it musters courage
breaking through its own hard shell.
Sparing no effort
it pushes forth two tender leaves
raising life's most captivating energy.

If it is the sprout of an oak,
do not fret its small stature
for one day
it will stand upon the earth and beneath the sky
bearing large gales and great snows
showing its vigour for life
reminding humanity—
use fortitude to face all challenges.

Cultivate

Where does one find joy and simplicity?

Cultivate your heart.

Within a sincere and pristine heart,
we may aspire to bring joy
to everyone around us.

If in this lifetime
and all lifetimes
fulfilling this dream is our only focus
then, how delightful and uncomplicated
would life be?

A Single Millet Becomes Thousands of Grains

Wishes are like seeds—
what you sow in spring
you will reap in autumn,
what you desire for in the future
you must wish for in the present!

Like the rain and sun
nourishing seeds sown in spring,
we must diligently gather merits
to sustain our seeds.

Planting a single grain of millet
may yield thousands in the autumn.
A beautiful kind heart,
with its lovely kind wishes,
will receive the most wonderful rewards.

What Can I Offer in This Moment

Many regrets and mistakes
happen when we are unaware.
Looking back, we see:
I have missed so many beautiful things!

But—
if in this time—
we choose to lament,
again,
we slight the beauty within this moment!

This moment, how precious the present moment.
What can I offer?

Elevating to a Higher Vantage Point

When we are stressed,
agonizing over a problem—
wrestling for answers—
a simple solution
is
prayer.

In prayer, we allow our heart to
rise above its current state,
bringing us to a higher vantage point.

With elevated wisdom,
we naturally know how to solve the problem at hand.

Beginning Where You Are

It doesn't matter how far behind you are—
instead—
courageously face the path before you.
Begin practicing from
exactly where you stand!
Remember
hold your head up high
because
all lives can only begin to change
by starting from exactly where they are.

Turning Obstacles into Opportunities

When someone yells at me,
I have a straightforward thought process:
Why do they say hurtful things?
Probably because in the past
I have also said hurtful things to them.
This is the karma coming into fruition.

I can also make an aspiration:
Because you have yelled at me,
We now have a connection on the path to enlightenment.
If I practice diligently,
I'll be able to help you in the future.

By turning our negative energy
into a positive driving force in the
pursuit of enlightenment,
we do not have to feel sadness or anger.

Kindness Brings Out Radiance

Ocean, because of its deep azure, brings beauty.
Forest, because of its green shades, brings tranquility.
Birds, because of their songs, bring joy.
As for me?
Training in the virtuous deeds and
ceasing the non-virtuous deeds,
my heart
because of its kindness
brings radiance.

Offering Our Hearts

Just like the coming of spring,
when so many flowers burgeon into full bloom,
a blossoming flower extends all its effort,
offering the world its own distinct fragrance.
Let us follow suit,
radiating like spring flowers,
offering our most sincere effort for others,
assisting them on their paths
away from suffering and toward happiness.
This desire is most precious.

As People of the Earth

We're not living amongst the silvery stars
but here on the beloved earth.
So let us engage in the issues on our earth—
our food, our soil, even our education.
We are all part of the planet and
responsible for its well-being.
Let's not wait passively for others to
solve our collective problems.

The Present Moment

We encounter one another
through many conditions from our past.
Within this cycle of saṃsāra,
it is remarkable that we can meet.
Inevitably, the day will come when we must part ways.
While we are gathered together
let us cherish these precious moments,
let us have goodwill in our hearts,
let us use our lives to truly benefit one another.

Where Strength Lies

Seeing a small critter,
though it may not recognize us,
we want it to be free of suffering and full of joy.
Taking this wish,
we can expand it—
may every living being be free of all suffering,
may every living being be full of all joy.
How do we develop the strength to
achieve these goals?
Attain enlightenment.

The Right Time

What does it mean to
observe the interplay of causes and conditions?

If we want to reason
with individuals who are starving
we
must
first
give
them
something
to eat.

Once they are settled, we can share our thoughts.
When we understand others,
recognize their needs,
and take care of their concerns.

This is being aware of
the causes and conditions
surrounding all things.

Sowing Aspirational Seeds

Though some things
cannot be accomplished now,

let us make aspirations.
An aspiration costs nothing.

Like walking along the sidewalk
scattering wildflower seeds
wait

come next year
flowers will spring.

Hope Is by You

The stars in the sky
a lighthouse at sea
the good in our hearts
all bring us hope.

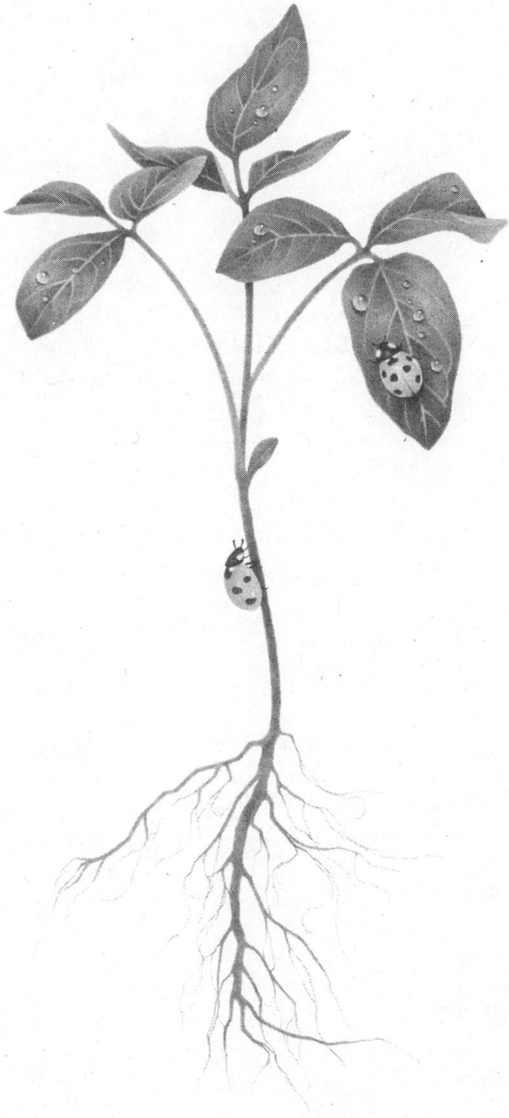

CHAPTER TWO

Nourishing the Midday Sapling

Springboard for Joy

It is not others' understanding or comfort
that is the basis for our happiness.
Instead, it is the love within our own heart
that is the springboard for our joy.

Stay the Course

Life—
like a boat sailing across the ocean
moving through the highs and lows,
we must stay the course
and steer toward our greatest dreams.
We can't be held back by our negativity and bias,
and we must not let the gales of suffering overturn us.

Becoming

How can a heart shine brightly?

If in all circumstances
our focus and our thinking reflect positivity,
then our words,
our thoughts, and
our actions
shine.

The Lingering Fragrance of Compassion

A compassionate heart is a happy heart,
for when we are compassionate to others
we will feel a deep sense of contentment.

Like the saying,

The
fragrance
always
lingers
on
the
hand
that
gives
the rose.

A Vow

Forever kindness—
I am committed.
Regardless of the difficulties and circumstances
even in the impossible
I will not let negative thoughts take root and sprout.

Let us safeguard the virtuous seed within us,
bright as the sun,
radiating like light,
the kind heart is
precious.

Choose to Be a Hero

Failure is just a feeling.

Overcoming it
again and again
is the hero's emblem.
Staying in hardship's mire
is also a choice.

The decision is ours.

Spreading Our Wings

If we use a proactive attitude
to face the challenge before us,
though it feels impossible,
this could be our moment
to surpass our limitations,
spread our wings and soar!

Working Through Our Troubles

When encountering difficulties, consider:
What is the situation I'm encountering?
In this situation, how am I reacting?
What may be the results of my reaction?

On the other hand, consider:
What is a more appropriate reaction to this situation?
What may be the results of this reaction?

After comparing both,
see which reaction brings the most joy and
stops the most suffering.

Choose that one.

Rousing Our Will

Sometimes even tiny situations,
insignificant as a grain of sand,
can shatter us.
But when we rally the strength in our hearts,
hardship becomes less hard.
This is the nature of our will!

Heart of a Learner

Once we tune our mind to be receptive to learning,
then no matter what circumstances we face
we will only count the lessons we have learned.
How have I enriched my heart?
How have I served others?
Our utmost concern will be
the harvest of our heart,
for it is said that
they who want to change the world
must first change their own heart.

Choose to Rise

In any situation,
always choose to rise—
just one step!
In time,
you'll develop the habit of being brave.

You'll know:
This too shall pass.
Difficulties are temporary,
I know because I've already overcome so many!
So, why can't I overcome this one?

Let Go of Failure

Feeling like a failure is a state of mind—
a state of mind is not a true reflection of all that I am.

A Clean Break from Our Fears

When faced with a challenge
some will want to find different excuses
to stay stagnant,
to run away,
or perhaps
to sink further into the distress,
refusing to rise.

In reality
this is an even bigger blow.
It's better to face the challenge head on and
find a solution.
It's best to cleanly break away from one's fears.

Get Lifted

When we are immersed in uplifting news,
don't we feel like we can just fly?

When we are swamped by disheartening news,
don't we feel like we can't walk or eat,
or even open our eyes?
How do we cast off the heart's burdens?

Inhale positivity
often.
Like leaves absorbing sunlight,
when facing situations
let's think proactively.
A positive way of thinking
greatly increases our immunity,
our mind and body become like a healthy little tree
surrounded by the sun,
grounded on the earth, and
overflowing with vitality.

Walking on Sunshine

When we encounter difficulties,
let's think:
Where is the silver lining?
When this thinking becomes a habit
we will become very brave and joyful,
as our eyes are always capable of finding beauty
finding things that bring light and
finding things that bring happiness.
When we are always searching for beauty
we subconsciously follow it.
Naturally
we walk in
beautiful brightness.

The Heart's Soft Winds

Soft winds
bring contentment.
Harsh winds,
heavy rains,
bring a refreshing release.

But the heart's angry winds
are like a hurricane passing through,
destroying forests of goodness,
sweeping cities of beauty.
Do not let it rise—
do not let it rouse!

Our heart's anger,
in two words—
Stop.
Extinguish.

Stir the gentle winds of
compassion and kindness
traveling in this world
bringing warmth to humanity.

Anger Needs Time

Words spoken in rage,
regret follows.

We have a tendency to solve conflicts while angry.
When anger is present,
the mind is compromised!
It's quick to judge and
its scope narrows,
making it hard to solve difficult problems.
Perhaps it's best to wait until our emotions have settled
to discuss solutions.
Because
with waiting
we become more effective and efficient,
less likely to hurt and be hurt.

A Gesture

Written in the gaze,
displayed on the face,
hidden within the words—
if we stop to look
we can find traces of another's sadness and pain.

When we notice a person is in such suffering,
can we think of something kind to say or do?
Perhaps
just a smile?

In that moment,
the world becomes more
beautiful.

Within Pain There is Growth

What does it mean to grow from pain?
Though we feel terrible suffering,
though we are helpless
in the face of external circumstances,
we can still choose to change our heart.
When we are suffering,
we can give rise to one positive thought:
For those who suffer as I do,
I shall strive to understand the true nature of suffering
to eliminate all of our pains.
This is an empowered way of thinking.
This way,
the pain we are experiencing
does not stunt our growth—
it is because of it
that we
grow.

A Hopeful Light

Within the darkness of saṃsāra,
let us spark the kindling in our hearts,
using our fires to send warmth to others,
inspiring them to ignite their own.
Together, let us endlessly care
for those who are undergoing distress.
When this power grows greater and greater,
one day this world will become paradise,
brimming with compassion and joy.

Fragile Hearts

The little ones
with their fragile hearts
interacting with them
we know this—

When we are angry
not to blurt out extreme words
that would hurt their tender hearts.

Veering on the safe side
not disciplining them when we are upset
as we might lose balance.

We wait until we've regained calm
and find a suitable way
to help them slowly learn.

Looking at the Road Ahead

Sometimes when I feel like others are offbeat
my eyes continually focus on them
and I want to correct them.

Inattention—even for just a second—and
not being aware of my own thoughts,
I trip on the big stones by my feet.
This is like having eyes but not seeing the road—
after a fall
I endure the injuries.

Look down,
walk steadily!
Look up,
into the distance!
Stay life's course.

Keeping On

Just when I feel like I'm never going to improve,
that's when I should keep on practicing.
The more familiarity I feel,
The faster I'll become.

When we begin to learn anything
we must first listen,
think,
then continuously practice
until we become a skillful master.

Trust the process.

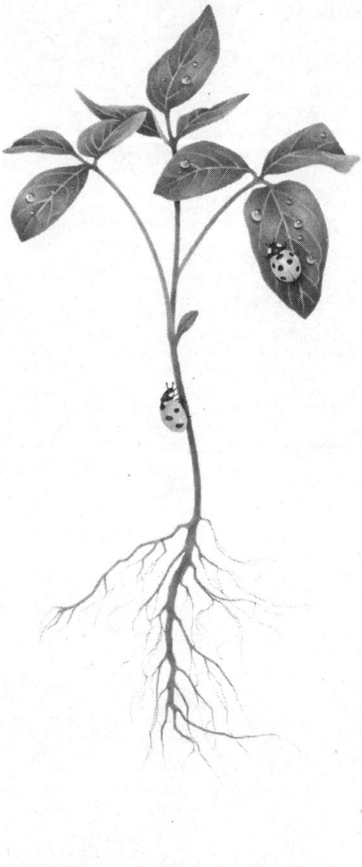

Mother Earth

Earth,
like a compassionate mother spreading her vast arms,
carries countless beings,
supporting their growth and their process of
birth, aging, sickness, and dying.
Like Mother Earth,
we also have the responsibility to protect other lives.

Whether due to carelessness
or an exaggerated sense of ourselves,
we may ignore the existence of other lives.
Let us try not to do this.

Living in this world together,
when we respect and embrace different ways of existing
we will feel harmony, joy, and
the pleasure of one another's company.

Defying Destiny

Face-to-face with difficulties
if we collapse and succumb
we can only cower before suffering.

Face-to-face with our troubles—
be they illness or complicated relationships—
if we step up
and rally ourselves to fight against fate,
we can defy destiny,
rising high above bad fortune.

Our Greatest Treasure: A Kind Heart

We do kind acts
not as displays for others to see
or as tokens for others' gratitude—
they are to transform our thoughts and actions.

Perhaps no one knows,
perhaps no one is thankful.
Some may take advantage the better you treat them,
others may even repay kindness with ire.

If this happens in our life—
calling into question our will to do good,
and we give up on our goal for goodness—
then this is the real disaster.
Losing our kind heart
hurts us far more than others' hostility.

We must not let
our kind heart be plundered by adversity.
It is our greatest treasure.

Constructions of the Mind

Joy and suffering are both constructions of the mind.
When others raise their voices,
when they do not acknowledge us,
when they twist words and misrepresent the truth,
why not use these circumstances
to create happiness and good karma?

Because all things are empty of intrinsic nature,
suffering and joy are dependent on
how the mind chooses to interpret them.

Weaving a Radiant World

When we approach each day
like creating a quilt,

our hearts are full of more positive thoughts,
our words are full of more kindness, and
our heartfelt gratitude is more often expressed.

Our collective karma will weave a world
abounding in radiant colours.
As our own suffering and joy
are tightly intertwined with those of others,

let us not allow our quilt
to become shabby and dirt-strewn,
or torn and destroyed
by negative karma.

Happy Practicing

Happiness—
is it only found in feelings?
Seeing past our immediate sensations,
guiding our mind into constructive thinking patterns—
can this methodically woven thought process
also give rise to joy?

For each endeavor,
embark with a meaningful and pure aspiration.
Throughout the process
be mindful of our thoughts, words, and actions.
Upon completion, for things we've done well, rejoice!
For things needing improvement,
reflect inwards, aspire to do better.
At the end,
dedicate all the goodness
from the kind acts that we have done
to the ultimate enlightenment of all beings.

With all this we can clearly see
ourselves forging ahead with courage
on this journey
of developing virtue and casting aside non-virtue.
Does this not bring joy?

Elusive Goodness

A person's elusive goodness,
like subtle flavours of tea,
lends itself to careful savouring,
taking time to appreciate its unique qualities.

Perchance the person
does not know how to or
desire to express themselves,
perchance they
only show their weaknesses.

Truly knowing another
is no easy task.
Only with extensive time
may one uncover
the beauty hidden
within.

A Reservoir for Warmth

How can a heart be full of warmth?
When it contains a reservoir of
compassion and gratitude
we should learn to use
kind acts and compassion toward others
to bring warmth to ourselves.
Only then will we readily love others.

For someone whose heart is bitter,
can they still show kindness to a child?
Yes. This practice is possible.

For someone whose heart is cold,
can they still care for an elderly person?
Yes. This practice is manageable.

For someone whose heart is broken,
can they still nurture a helpless animal?
Yes. This practice is feasible.
In fact, they may become the animal's only source of support.

It is in the process of caring for others
that we discover our own worth.

You and I are capable of kindness.
We are like flowers,
some radiating sweetness,
others tinged with bitterness,
while still others hint at elegance.
Every flower is different,
but all aromas bring joy.

Fiery Mountain, Cooling Ocean

When others rise in rage, I rise in compassion.
I shall use my compassion
like water against the flames of anger.
Who will prevail?
They may be resolved to rage.
I am resolved to compassion.
If anger is a fiery mountain,
compassion is the cooling ocean.

The Road to Virtue

It is unrealistic to expect ourselves to change overnight.
No one reaches their goals immediately.
With time and effort
our habits become better than they were.
This is remarkable!
A positive change—even a small one—
is fought for with sweat and tears.
Do not discount our hard work.
Virtue is collected one grain at a time
until
one day
we are entirely virtuous.

Strive

It's not always easy to do good.
In these moments, the heart must first change.

In gentle winds and bright skies
acts of kindness are
beautiful and warm.
In harsh winds and heavy rains
acts of kindness are
even more resplendent
like a rainbow after a storm.
Therefore,
one need not falter.
Oh,
doer of good,
continue!

Introspection

In this moment,
we must know what our mind is thinking,
recognize what our lips are saying,
be mindful of what our body is doing.

We must sharpen the skill of self-awareness,
which allows us to carefully observe the mind.
When the mind is directed at hurting others,
we become a trainer
masterfully taming the beast within.
Only in thoroughly eliminating
self-harm and harming others
through body, speech, and mind
may we truly attain happiness.

Colliding

Washing a giant pile of potatoes,
one potato at a time, takes a long time.
If you gather all the potatoes into a pail,
pour in water, and stir,
they collide, quickly becoming clean.
Everyone has different strengths and weaknesses.
By rubbing shoulders,
colliding, and
learning from one another,
many issues quickly resolve!

The Power of Words

Language—
our thoughts in flight
connected
one after the other.
Where our intentions lie
our words soon follow
leading us
there.
Where our thoughts fly
our life soon
follows.

Enjoying the Calm of Reading

On airplanes,
you'll discover that some people
always have a book in their hands.
In parks, under great trees, on long benches,
some are always enraptured,
savouring the taste of the words on the page.
Their expressions are so focused,
they seem like part of a painting—
quiet, serene,
even
joyful.

Training Our Thought Rivers

In wishing to achieve
life's profoundest tranquility and bliss,
I must turn inward
to battle the muddled perspectives within.

Trains of thought
that have not undergone rational analysis
are like rivers with overflowing banks—
they lead to disaster.

Hurt Can't Take Away Happiness

Though you've been hurt,
you still have the right to be happy.
This right belongs to you and you alone,
no one can take it away.

Rewriting Memories

Can memories be rewritten?
After a difficult time,
even though our heart overflows with pain,
can we learn to grow from this suffering?
Find some hope and gather your harvest.
Do not let suffering cause you distress in vain.
In life, one must grow to learn and learn to grow.

Bedrock to Happiness

Wisdom is the wealth I most desire,
the teacher and friend I cannot abandon,
the light I cannot stray from,
the mountain I will always rely on.
I shall never surrender my pursuit of wisdom
because wisdom is essential to happiness.

Perseverance

On your journey, start with your first steps and
learn as fast as you are able, but as slowly as you need.
Earnestly and conscientiously take one step at a time.
Even if you are the slowest walker
as long as you never stop
perseverance is your most precious treasure—
one day
you
will
succeed.

Unclouded Lens

With the haze removed from our lens
we see the wonders of the world.
Developing our self and bringing light to our heart
we see the wonders within.
When we clearly see what is within—
even if we notice a flaw
or how we need to change—
it is a wondrous scene of discovery and awakening.

A Forgotten Comfort

Summers in the north,
the wind carries the sweet smell of flowers,
softly skimming past mountains,
softly skimming past fields,
softly skimming past people.
How long since we've truly smelled the flowers,
and felt the gentle breeze brushing our face?

Living in buildings of concrete and metal,
with a computer as our partner,
do not forget nature's fresh air and warm sunlight—
they will comfort our heart.
Come outside.
Walk.

Love, As Clear as Spring

If winter passes
but the grasses are not green,
the willows are not budding,
the flowering trees are not blooming,
will it feel like spring?

With sincerity,
we can explicitly express love to our family,
otherwise,
how can they truly feel our warmth?
How can we melt animosity after an argument?

Spring expresses so clearly—
the grasses are now green,
the flowers are now red,
the water is now trickling.

As for us,
how are we expressing?

Learn to Admire Your Brilliance

We should learn to admire our own heroic journey. Growth often secretly happens in the deepest crevices of our heart. From the outside we may look like a disaster at times, but in truth we are waging the most heroic war within, battling and struggling bravely.

This is a truly magnificent process.

The Power of One Sincere Thought

Even if one only recites this mantra once:
Om mani padme hum

if it is recited for all sentient beings
with the aspiration for all
to leave suffering and attain happiness,
if it is earnestly recited for every single being—
because they are infinite and countless
our merits are infinite and boundless.

Dear Practitioner

You are a warrior.

Battling against our afflictions
perception is a sword
we must draw it quickly!

How quickly can we catch our afflictions?
Compared to the us of yesterday,
how many thoughts run through our mind
before we recognize our negative thoughts?
After we notice
can we immediately stop them?

We must train to
quickly draw our sword!

This is the key to success!

Steeped in Compassion

The wind sweeps by one with compassion,
shuffling its strength and
sprinkling it onto the next person,
skimming it into the trees and
sliding it into the fields—
the grasses and woods,
all steeped in the splendor of compassion.

Lose and Gain

When we feel great suffering,
do we choose to act out and hurt others,
or do we choose to endure it,
enhancing our own virtues instead?

On the surface,
though the latter may appear as if we've lost out,
after this trying ordeal
we'll discover:
When I am facing difficulties,
I can insist on choosing kindness!
I can cultivate virtue!

In the end
we gain far more.

Always a Warrior

When we have afflictions,
though we want to create virtuous karma,
we might not have autonomy.
Precisely because of this,
we must continue to strive—
pies don't simply fall from the sky.
Every ounce of cultivation is gained through struggle.

With unshakeable determination
we challenge our afflictions 24/7
until they crumble.

Though we often may not succeed
we never give up!
We are always fighters!

Warriors of constant defeat,
though we fall
we always rise again.

Calm Within the Storm

Anxiety will make problems more complicated,
even causing them to spread like disasters.

When we are facing a difficult situation
we must first keep calm
before observing how to overcome it.

Something Counterintuitive

When we are feeling dreary,
is there anything we can do?

Let's try something counterintuitive:
Lend a helping hand.
We will find that our low spirits quickly dissipate.
Give this a try and we'll discover
cultivating compassion is the way.

Walking with Gratitude

A clean environment
stems from others' hard work.
As we walk into our building,
the floor beneath our feet
is swept by others,
and when others are sweeping,
though they may be sweating
and though their backs may ache,
walking upon this floor,
we can be mindful of these efforts.
This cleanliness,
let us cherish and protect it.

Fruits of Two Kinds

Can we place ourselves in others' shoes?

Immersed in our own feelings,
how can we understand the feelings of others
whose experiences are completely different
from our own?

Like the apple growing in the chilly north
wondering
what the durian fruit in the tropical south thinks.
If the apple only thinks within temperatures of the north
it will never understand the durian's life.

Let go of yourself,
wholeheartedly.
listen.
If I were you
what would I do?

In this way,
can we better understand others' feelings?
Wholeheartedly explore,
and learn from those who know.

Holding Up the Sun

Teachers—
it is as if they are lifting the sun
as they protect the power that light and justice bring,
holding it
growing it
within the hearts of students
from generation to generation,
passing it still further
into our future generations.
Allowing this world to be warm,
allowing this world to shine brightly,
this is a sacred profession.

24/7

What is the purpose of observing the mind?
To cast aside what is harmful,
to choose what is beneficial.

There is a Buddhist saying:
"Twenty-four hours a day and seven days a week,
we only need to observe the mind,
for what else must be done?"

Can I not be lazy or lax,
and make overcoming afflictions
my utmost priority?

As a practitioner,
grounding each step of my practice,
steadfastly transforming my karma
is most important.

Becoming a Cause for Hope

Compassion's fragrance floats
like scent wafting over a field of flowers,
swayed by the winds of beautiful wishes,
bringing more positive news into a weary world,
allowing humanity's joy and contentment to
continually grow.
Oh, may we all become a cause for
joy and hope in the world!

CHAPTER THREE

Burgeoning in the Dusk

The Burgeoning Garden Within

Gazing at a flower in the summer breeze
softly swaying.
Gentleness—
like the flower's soft fragrance—
from our eyes
from our smile
rippling
it spreads.

Burgeoning gardens are
like the heart's kind thoughts—
when they blossom within
the whole person radiates
bringing compassion
into the
world.

Home to All

Our faith can allow our heart to become
a source of light in this world.

Our compassion can become
a source of refuge in others' lives.

Like a large tree countless birds flock to—
whether they love to belt their high-pitched songs
or prefer their timbred chimes,
wearing white, black, and rainbows too,
all covered in an assortment of hues.
Everyone is welcome—
animals as large as the eagle and
insects as small as the ant,
because there is a great tree
where they all come together,
they all call it
home.

Seeing Through the Shadows

The larger our heart, the larger our world.

If we live solely for ourselves,
even in the brightness of the sun
we will see only our shadow.

When our heart is filled with other people,
we will naturally think about sharing
our warmth and love.

Without a second thought, we think,
I want to give forth my efforts to others!

Recognizing Sincerity

For a while, stand in other people's shoes.
Experience their sincerity and
reflect on the things they have done for you,
be it daily tasks or times of support.
Perhaps these things seem insignificant,
but know that in those moments
they did them
wholeheartedly
for you.

Enjoying Conversations

In the unrelenting pace of life,
pour a cup of tea,
sit with your family and talk.
Smile as you listen to how they are doing,
hear what may be bothering them,
compliment them on their improvements.

Having someone close to us nursing a cup of tea,
smiling as they listen to us speak—

don't you think in these moments
sitting with someone like this,
we slowly release our stresses and
find peace and joy.

Adjusting the Heart's Strings

A violin's strings
must be neither too tense nor too loose,
to play beautiful melodies.
Anxiety—
are strings too tight?
Carefully adjust,
do not simply forge ahead,
rushing.
Observe yourself—
in this state, can I maintain my pace
walking for long
while trying to avoid mistakes?

Flexibility and resilience
are learned through adjustments
made again and again.
If you are often on the brink of collapse,
consider heartstrings—
are they too tense?

A Light, a Friend, a Guide

What is a teacher?

Drowning in darkness,

a teacher is our light.

Isolated in loneliness,

a teacher is our friend.

Lost in confusion,

a teacher is our guide,

helping us understand
what to adhere to,

and what must be released.

Home is the Cradle of Peace

We all hope for world peace, but where does it begin?

Peace starts in the home.
With a little more compromise, and
a little more gratitude,
life is more joyful.

Spring of Happiness

A heart of gratitude is like the sun
bringing warmth to our lives.
Like a freshwater spring
it brings nourishment to our hearts.
It is the elixir of happiness
our lives cannot be without.

Riches in Gratitude

There is a saying:
Gratitude is riches. Complaint is poverty.

As we develop a grateful heart,
we will see the bigger picture:
At this moment,
how many people,
how many lives,
are contributing to the well-being of all?

Recognizing all good things come from effort,
we can't help but be grateful.

An Open Heart

Amidst the dynamics of
our interpersonal relationships,
whether with loved ones,
teachers and students,
people we work with—
acknowledge and appreciate
the kind intentions of others,
communicate with an open heart.

When we do this throughout our lives
we can truly experience how
leaving suffering and finding happiness happens
before our very eyes.
Perhaps it's not as hard as we think.

Increasing Inner Strength

As our heart becomes more and more powerful,
we can take on challenges of
greater and greater magnitude—
after we surmount these difficulties,
our heart grows stronger still!
Our strength grows until we eventually
extinguish all suffering in saṃsāra.

Spurring Change

I hope all of us can work together
to make this world a more beautiful place!
Even if our efforts happen under a dim lamp,
facing one other person,
voicing a few words of gratitude
despite the coldest of winters,
a sentence spoken in kindness
will still warm the heart.
In truth,
the world will change because of our gratitude.

Let's spur this change by
expressing our gratitude to those around us!

A Heartfelt Education

The part of us
that focuses on the joys and sorrows of others,
let us strive to nurture it,
to become ever more true and ever more noble.

Slowly, our relationships will begin to evolve,
and we can touch the lives of others.
In reality
it simply means to use one's
body, speech, and mind to uplift and inspire.
Like a summer's breeze,
this can bring warmth to dreary hearts,
and the courage to do good.
This way,
even when they meet with obstacles,
they have the strength to carry on.

Warrior of Constant Defeat

I am often defeated
but why am I a warrior and not a deserter?
I know if I never give up
I will win this battle,
I will surpass this hardship and eventually
I will destroy the roots of all suffering in saṃsāra.

Blindfolded

What we can see is limited,
what we can hear is finite—
if we only depend on
what we can see with our eyes and hear with our ears
without utilizing logic and reasoning
to explore the world,
it's as if our lives are trapped,
locked in our own reality.

Change the Channel

Memories,
using the mind to recall a situation—
the images, the sounds, the thoughts—
do we tend to watch tragedies or fairy tales?

If we often watch tragedies,
after replaying them
do we feel more rage and heartache?
Do we want someone to pay?

Spending our time
remembering others' wrongs,
does it ruin our own day?

If we notice ourselves replaying a tragedy,
quickly—
stop!
Change the channel,
start a voyage of joy and kindness.

A wondrous destination
or a dreadful one
is your heart's prerogative.

Letting Go of the Ego

If we only focus on and care about ourselves,
thinking that we are the most important,
then the little challenges around us
will feel like a thousand bristles.
That's what happens when we indulge the ego—
endless pitfalls.
But if we slightly shift our gaze
and start to pay closer attention to others,
perhaps to even more lives in the world,
prioritizing their troubles and joy
and helping out when needed—
perhaps the situation hasn't changed,
but we may feel better.
Then we will witness our growth
in every situation!

Infusing Sincerity

How many times do we reply to
others' messages each day?

If in all our replies
we have a pure aspiration
infused with sincerity
may all things be wonderful!

This is also a kind of
inner cultivation.

What Can I Offer?

When we use eyes of gratitude
to gaze in all directions
we unearth:
trees offering their cool shade,
flowers offering their fresh fragrance,
parents offering their great love.

And I—
what can I offer in return?

A Time Without Regret

A thousand-mile sky
clear and untainted
geese in formation
vigorously fly.
Where is my heart's home?

Small things notwithstanding
great trials notwithstanding
human life is precious.
In time's softly flowing river
how many things are done
without a trace of regret?

Grateful Eyes

The things that happen regularly,
do I notice them?
Mother, making me breakfast every day,
teacher, teaching me lessons every day,
the sun, moon, and stars bringing me light every day—
if I can use a pair of grateful eyes
to look at life,
how much warmth and happiness
will live in my
heart?

The Most Precious Thing

No matter what you encounter,
be it suffering
be it happiness
be it the compliments of others
or even their criticisms,
when you meet with opportunities to help,
do not forget the heart that wants to offer assistance.
Though methods
must be carefully considered,
a heart that truly wants to help
can be
a precious gift.

Let's Take Action

Right now,
perhaps we can express our apologies.
Maybe with a phone call or a visit,
use our most genuine heart,
our most gentle demeanor, saying:
"I was wrong, I'm sorry! Please don't be sad!"

Right now,
perhaps we can find a way to express our gratitude
with a phone call or a card,
take the gratitude in our heart
and give it to the eyes and ears of those
we're thankful for.

Don't wait,
don't find excuses,
because
the time to act is now!

Untangling Challenges

The more anxious we are,
the more tangled our thoughts,
the more unlikely we are to find a solution.

When our heart calms,
it grows more encompassing
and new solutions rise
to the challenges before us.

Finding Common Ground

This world is full of more and more stress and anxiety,
so when having discussions and interacting with others
try to avoid putting them under more pressure.
First, find the common goal,
then discuss the differences.
This can be a powerful way to start discussions.

Silent Bookkeeping

You should've said hello, but you didn't.
You should've helped, but you didn't.
You should've bought gifts, but you didn't.
You should've said those words, but you didn't.

In our books,
we keep a clear record of all the debts they owe us,
but when debt endlessly accumulates and
is taking its toll,
wouldn't we want repayment?
How do we plan on exacting it?
Have we considered the aftermath?

An Unwelcome Act

Sometimes when we make a mistake
we start to say things about others
to put them down.

Do we do this to protect ourselves
or because we are afraid of others
hearing about what we've done?
But others can't be fooled,
so if we replay this act often
people will slowly start to recognize:
Oh... you have a habit of spreading rumours!
Our reputation solidifies.
This destructive habit is not wise.
We should take responsibility for our own actions,
as we cannot use crushing rumours
to demonstrate our innocence.

A Dark Cloud

A nervous, angry face
makes others stressed
and fearful.
One person's anxiety
can make all people around them
agitated.

Take a deep breath,
adjust your nerves, and
transform
from a cloud of darkness
into a ray of light.

Kindness Snowflakes

Pure white, delicate snowflakes
blossom by blossom
drift down from the sky,
descending.
Every snowflake
so light and small,
how can one imagine that
together they will blanket the earth?
Slowly covering
rooftops, forests
until the whole world is an expanse of silver white.

Our kind thoughts
though small
though light,
endlessly rising and rising,
will, too, envelop our mind,
creating a purely kind heart,
a purely kind world.

The Lion Within

When we are in a challenging situation
and cannot find help
or the help we anticipate harms us instead,
like when we are on a battlefield
and our own soldiers rebel
we are left battered and beaten.
Though it is so,
while we still have breath,
let's not forget the strength we have within.

By learning and gaining truth
as soon as our inner strength awakens
we will discover the lion within.

Our only task is:
through learning,
awaken the lion.

Self-Clarity

You say, "A."
I say, "B."
You say, "I'm right."
I say, "You're wrong."

Within all these discussions and disagreements
what have we actually gained?

Can we find clarity within,
like the bright moon
illuminating the night?

How does deep and powerful calm arise?

Let's evaluate our own lives,
especially our ways of thinking.
Life is complicated—
we must continue to
deeply reflect and discern.

Steps Toward Change

Changing the world begins by
changing our heart.
Changing our heart begins by
changing our understanding.

Changing our actions begins by
cultivating mindfulness in every situation.
Cultivating right mindfulness begins by
noticing the presence of our afflictions
in all that we find ourselves in.

Building Trust

If we often advocate for everyone to
help others and be considerate
yet overlook our own inner practice,
allowing our actions and thoughts to slip,
we can sense that we are not being true to ourselves.

If we cannot practice self-discipline,
how are we to model it for others?
If our actions don't match our words,
how can we build trust?

A Compassionate Milieu

All human beings
and even animals
hope to live in a compassionate atmosphere—
nobody wants to live in an indifferent world.

So why don't we
create compassion!
Create gratitude!
Create forgiveness!

Let's enthusiastically create a world
full of these beautiful qualities.
Let's rise to this responsibility!

Collecting Grains of Gold

If we are continuously changing for the better
this is enough.
If we are continuously changing in a positive direction,
even if we are only improving a little bit,
our steps are precious.
Because how much sweat and how many tears
have we exchanged for them?

Do not overlook little changes,
because like sifting for gold in a river,
even if acts of goodness are as small as a grain of sand,
they are still gold.

Being Where You Stand

We should notice the steps we have already taken
because if our eyes are always looking
down the road we have yet to tread
at the things we have yet to complete
will we accumulate anxiety and frustration?

Without realizing it
we start to complain about ourselves
as we start to notice flaws everywhere else as well
and complain about others.
Why?
Because we are in such a hurry wanting to be efficient.

In the moments
when we should be evaluating our heart
we are always thinking about what is to come next,
ignoring our opportunities to observe—
this is also a kind of "wasting time."

The journey of cultivation
cannot be rushed and cannot be slowed—
our speed must be just right
so we may steadily
and continuously walk.

Not Set in Stone

Prayer can change the direction of
our karma and perspective on problems.
With a perspective change
many problems unravel.
Our greatest obstacle lies in
the stubborn attachment that
in this moment
at this time
this situation is
set in stone
absolute and unchanging.
Therefore,
a change in mindset
can give our thoughts the freedom and space to soar.

Mastery from Extended Practice

Accumulate more and more experience
taming the mind.
Practice—
ten years,
twenty years,
lifetime after lifetime—
and you will become a master.

Seasoned practitioners know exactly how to handle the afflictions within their minds.

From Distress to Peace

Are our lives filled with joy,
or are our lives filled with distress?
Who decides?

A practitioner decides for themselves.

Whether we want to live a pessimistic and despairing life,
or one with joy, compassion, and wisdom,
the decision is entirely in our hands.
Like training our muscles
training our mind allows it to grow strong.
Then,
not only will we transform our worries into peace,
we'll have the strength to
support others through their hardships.

CEO of Life

If our life was a company,
we would be the CEO
of this life and our infinite lives.

We get to decide:
work for immediate benefits,
or look further into the future for even greater returns?

As our eyes, ears, nose, tongue, body, and mind
run our company,
the higher our vantage point,
the more successful we will be.

Our Strongest Tool

The ability to contemplate
is like having a diamond drill bit.
It drives us to transcend our feelings
so we can immerse ourselves in life's most profound logic.

Slowly,
we can peel ourselves away from
our tendency to believe in how things appear.

Observe truth.
This observation brings the strength of piercing insight,
allowing us to face life's illusion head on.

Unwavering Amidst Wavering

In the process of battling our afflictions
no matter how many times we fail
we must fight until the end!

Even if we duel to our last breath,
we can break free from
the bonds of our negative karma
we can defeat our negative habits!
As long as we hold true to this mindset—
unwavering—
our afflictions and our negative karma
will certainly waver.

The Mark of the Hero

To put up with others,
to endure some unfairness,
to control your actions, words, and thoughts,
and not plant negative karma—
this is the true mark of the hero!

The ability to tame one's heart,
to thoroughly conquer oneself,
this person is the greatest hero!

The Free Practitioner

Diligently practice—
month after month, year after year—
until one experiences the freedom of a true practitioner.
To flourish
one no longer depends on material things
or expects the accommodation and
admiration of others.

And in all circumstances
naturally within the heart
this thought arises:
How can I benefit and respect others?

This practitioner's heart is like a summer garden
flourishing with life!
No matter how the rain pours
the flowers radiate beauty,
because unwavering kindness raises their petals—
unhindered
they fearlessly bloom.

Forever Standing

In the most intolerable times
enduring,
striving,
refusing to cower to negative karma—
non-virtuous actions of the body, speech, and mind—
this is the practitioner's greatest victory.

Connecting with Others

When we genuinely foster understanding between people,
we can work together to create goodness.

Learn to communicate with others,
to understand their needs,
to know when they need assistance, and
to provide it.

Like the warm wind brushing through spring trees—
everyone wants to
see the burgeoning fair flowers
of understanding and
feel the caressing soft winds
of consideration.

A Bodhisattva's Heart

We can train an altruistic heart,
practicing diligently so it is
brighter, stronger, and purer.
When we are with others, we can think:

I wish to bring you happiness.

With this liberating mindset
we step forward.

We can walk toward others ten thousand times,
they may turn away ten thousand times,
But we will still march forward for
the ten-thousand-and-first time.

The problem is not others,
it's that we've yet to find a method
to connect with them.

Bestowing the Light of Compassion

Amidst our anguish
we have a choice:
sink more deeply into our woes
or give rise to a different train of thought—
we can immediately think of all beings
who are suffering like us.

I hope to offer all beings
fruits from my good karma—
happiness and joy, completely free of suffering.
I aspire to bear the burdens of their suffering.

The moment this kind of thought arises,
a ray of light beams in the darkness.

Wait—
the light will grow
until it becomes as bright as the sun.
Full of compassion
it will light the ocean of suffering.
Every drop of water
will brim with compassion—
catching our eyes
becoming an ocean of illumination.

The Power of the Team

Those who can reach the pinnacle of the mountain
are champions,
because only those with courage can reach the top.

But, in deeply connected teams
many champions are born.

All ardently love the team,
reluctant for any one person to leave,
and so support those who are less strong,
inspiring courage!

The best teamwork is everyone
climbing and reaching the summit together.

Helping Others is Helping Ourselves

All things we do to help other beings
actually always help ourselves.
Sometimes it may look like we are on the losing end,
but in reality we are gaining,
we are letting go of
an unhealthy habit of self-centeredness—
a tendency that only brings
unhappiness and untold regrets.
So, why not consider leaving it behind
and insist on helping others?

Pondering

At this moment,
are there people suffering more than I am?
What support may I offer them?

At the same time,
what are the people around me thinking about?
What can I do for them?

Vibrant Blossoms

When many kind and virtuous people
gather together to help not only one another,
but also complete strangers,
this will bring warmth to the world—
like fragrant flowers,
vibrantly blossoming in the universe.

Gathering Where the Books Are

When stopping by a friend's house
what room do you most want to see?
I always want to see the room filled with books.

When everyone is together
with a book in hand
quietly reading—
these encounters are a different kind of delight.

Karma: One Must Act

In misfortune, to sigh and blame
wastes precious time and makes us
even more miserable.

Why not proactively think—
what are the causes for suffering?
How can I eliminate them?
Destiny is in our own hands.
Karma states:
One must act!

The Magnolia

The magnolias bloom
large blossoms
pearl-white and shining on verdant branches,
under the sun,
even more resplendent.
When we master the cultivation of joy,
we are also as the magnolia tree—
pure, serene joy
burgeoning on our branches
burgeoning in our life.

CHAPTER FOUR

Old Growth Under Midnight Skies

Cascade

In darkness
a tiny flicker of light still burns—
no matter how small, a good deed is a light in our lives.
Even if there is only a humble glimmer of light,
its sparkle can illuminate us and shine upon others,
bringing warmth.
This glimmer of light,
when strung together with other sprinklings of light,
will become a vivid ocean of lights.
Within a cascade of lights, how can darkness prevail?

Beauty in Withering

This winter, a thick layer of snow covers the earth.

As I'm standing by the window
a bird is standing in the snow,
vigorously pecking at a dry, wilted flower.
Are there seeds?
I wonder.
The bird eats,
enjoying its feast.
Standing there I realize:
Even a wilted flower has its worth,
providing for birds in winter's dearth.

The Flow of Time

Causes and conditions are endlessly changing.
As for our lives,
moment by moment our thoughts are changing.
Amidst all of this
we can direct life's flow toward happiness.
Our hands cannot hold on to the past—
perhaps by releasing our past gloom
we can notice,
now
I can create many opportunities for joy.

Oh! It Was a Blessing

Sometimes when blessings come knocking
we feel inexplicable sadness, or a desire to retreat
because the situation may appear
upsetting, painful, or threatening
but
looking back
we discover:
Oh! It was actually wonderful!

Let us not hastily draw conclusions regarding the situations before us.

Faith Brings Strength

Faith directs the path of our heart,
inspiring compassion and wisdom,
bringing happiness and strength into our life.

As time passes and
we become more adept at our practice,
the bindings of the afflictions
that once so entangled us,
slowly begin to loosen.

Confronted with misfortune and injury,
though not a soul offers us comfort or apology,
we are imbued with the strength to uplift ourselves—
we will not suffocate, trapped within our woes.

We
are
powerful.

Solace in Faith

When we are afflicted by sickness
beyond what we can endure,
when medicine no longer helps,
when family's comfort no longer brings solace,
what can we rely on?
Faith.
A heart that prays!
One can be ill,
one can draw on the last breath,
but one need not suffer so.

Though we may not be completely at ease
on the torturous waves of illness,
we can wield our positive thoughts and
gracefully dance upon their swells.

The Torch of Communication

Building harmony requires our all.

Within saṃsāra,
rather than wasting time
wallowing and being frustrated,
it is better if
within the darkness
we raise the torch of communication.

Calm our minds and listen.

Antagonism melts away
if we can first understand others,
creating channels of communication.

What is the best antidote for conflict?
Compassion.

Reframing Our Hurt

When you've been hurt
by someone else's wrongdoings,
you may feel like you'll never heal,
especially when you've given your all.
Being let down,
being lied to,
these painful wounds within—
how can you start to heal?
How can you be free?

You have to think of ways to minimize your hurt.
At the very least
the situation is over.
You don't have to keep replaying your memories,
each revisit another nightmare.
This unconscious process
is like rubbing salt into your wounds.

Recognize:
In this process,
I keep replicating my hurt.

So first—
press pause on the memories.

Allow the mind to extract itself.
You can read,
do kind deeds,
care for others,
even care for a stray animal!
There are always kind things you can do.
At the very least
this is a more worthwhile way to live.

Notice It and Break Free

Why do we stick to our afflictions?
Because we believe we have reason,
not thinking they need to be addressed.
Perhaps
we don't think they're afflictions at all!

The deeper we delve into afflictions
the harder they are to
overcome.

Perhaps
the most essential key to overcoming our afflictions is
noticing them
knowing their faults
and then
at lightning speed
breaking away from them.

We can stop the spiraling.

Finding Closure and Peace

When we are unable to find a reason to forgive,
we can use this line of reasoning:
they experience the suffering of saṃsāra,
they are overcome with the suffering of afflictions.

With this,
we can find forgiveness.

Success Is Yours

Do not fear,
do not hesitate,
do not retreat.
Forge onwards
and success will be yours.
If you're headed in the right direction
why shouldn't happiness be yours?

Take Notice

Taking a moment to notice
the circumstances of the people in our surroundings,
we realize:
I'm actually quite blessed!

Many are enduring aches,
experiencing difficulties, emotionally and physically,
struggling in their families and relationships,
stretched so thin,
already beyond their limits.
In these situations,
can we offer a little bit of warmth to support them?

Flowing Toward the Ocean of Enlightenment

Though some of the good deeds we do upon the earth
may seem as insignificant
as droplets of rain,
when we gather them and
they flow
toward the ocean of enlightenment
their effects never end.

The Strong Have Patience, the Brave Forgive

In truth
patience and forgiveness are not cowardice,
they belong to a valiant heart—
brave and magnanimous.
Like the tranquil ocean,
quiet and magnificent,
soothing and powerful.
Like a strong warrior,
with a gentle smile.

Rising Above

Sometimes in our lives, we encounter a harsh blow, whether by others' doing or our own. We find ourselves falling into an endless abyss—both helpless and hopeless.

All becomes darkness.
But giving up is no solution.

Is there a way to find our bearings
to welcome rock bottom?

The bottom is our vantage point—our new horizon—from which both darkness and light emerge. The sun sets below the horizon, the sun rises above the horizon.

From where we fall,
we shall rise again.

Restoring Calm Waters

The constant bias toward the self
stirs the calm waters of the mind.
From the day-to-day to the life-changing
the habit of blaming the external—
instantly triggered—
fires relentlessly and spirals out of control,
but the more we grasp, the more we suffer.

Instead,
if the moment we encounter a situation
we learn to direct our focus within,
to strike against our self-centeredness,
we will find peace.

Triumphing in Darkness

What brings more exhilaration
than the eradication of darkness?
I shall tackle suffering and not let it suppress me!
With this fierce determination
our heart grows stronger and stronger, and
our life shines brighter and brighter.
Hardships will not destroy us,
instead,
it is precisely because of hardships that
we triumph.

Happiness Through and Through

If you practice being aware and mindful
of your heart every day,
then at eighty, ninety, or even one hundred,
you will still be happy!
Let aging be aging, I am still happy!
The older I am, the happier I become.
Let sickness be sickness, I am still joyful!
Lying in bed, I can still be happy!

Distancing from Anger

Overcoming the anger within
is so much easier than changing others!

The moment we start on this path
we open the door to happiness, and
walk further and further from the curse of anger.

Firefly

Even if I am only a firefly, beaming a little light,
I aspire to shine upon others' paths,
so that in their hearts they see their paths,
knowing what to follow and what to forsake.

The Light of Compassion

Compassion is like a beam of light,
driving away the ghosts of loneliness and pain.

A compassionate person
opens their heart to the universe.
The universe's light
scatters in.

Courage in Apologies

In our hearts,
if we do not feel apologetic when we make mistakes,
or, if we do, but lack the courage to apologize,
we cannot simply let it be.
Repentance is a wonderful practice that
generates great merit.
So, it is essential for us to use it!

Making or Breaking

The more a selfish heart may desire,
the more deprived it becomes.
The dreams we so desire
one after another
evade us.
Our lives become more and more barren.

The more altruism a heart desires,
the more encompassing it becomes.
The dreams we so desire
one after another
arise.

The Charm of Softness

Soft coloured interiors
offer calm to the emotions.
A soft expression
offers comfort to the heart.

Life Passes

Fighting every day,
hating each other every day,
is a way to live our lives.
Smiling every day,
having gratitude for each other every day,
is another way.
So why not face others with happiness every day?

Time, like the wind, rushes past us.
How many days do we still have together?
Let us not leave too many regrets,
let us leave gratitude instead.

The Power of Warmth and Light

Within the dark night,
we are walking together.
One heart lighting another heart,
the darkness becomes bright.
With more and more hearts
our effects become greater and greater.
The power of our warmth
radiates
within our whole society,
our whole world, and
our whole universe!

Sheltering Hope's Light

Let us not only protect the goodness within ourselves,
but let us also protect and inspire
the goodness in others.
As humans,
being in this world,
this is the most beautiful thing.
Encouraging ourselves and others
to become more kind and more compassionate,
is like carrying a bright light,
forever spreading
hope.

Toward Inner Peace

Self-centeredness is a habit
that has developed through long years of practice.
Likewise, other-centeredness is also a habit
that can be developed through practice.
The key is:
We have to be willing.

In the beginning
would we be keen on it?
Maybe not.

But if you truly want to change your life,
refusing to accept a life without inner peace,
perhaps we can try practicing in this direction!

Cherishing Like New

During the mid-autumn festival,
people join together to see the full moon.
Every year,
people are still in awe.
They do not fret, saying,
"Why has the same moon come again?"

Relationships between people
who have been together for a long time
can still be cherished like new.

Let us use our heart
to help those we love through their unhappiness.
Let us use our heart
to help them find joy.

The Gift of Serenity

A serene heart masterfully creates and nurtures
an extraordinary and courageous strength.
Within a heart without distractions,
in moments of utmost serenity,
the things we often cannot parse
suddenly become crystal clear.
Gratitude and compassion,
as well as the power to explore the wisdom of emptiness,
will also easily arise in our heart.

Shining Light

As long as the lighthouse on the shore shines,
the boats in the water will not lose their way.
As long as the heart's mindful compass shines,
the path beneath our feet will not stray.

Happy Living

When helping another and benefiting ourselves
come into conflict,
perhaps we can choose to put others first.
This choice is a happy one.
If you're skeptical,
try it!

And don't try just once or twice,
and reach a conclusion—
keep trying
ten years, twenty years
continue on—
one day we will realize,
making others our priority
is the happiest way to live.

Way of the Practitioner

On our journey toward enlightenment
I hope we can be familiar with a way of thinking:

I will find the source of my problems within,
and then I will find ways to resolve them.

This is the way of the practitioner.

Facing Our Greatest Adversity

There is no adversity that cannot be overcome
through inner practice!

Even death—
the pain that all living beings dread most—
with true cultivation,
in the process of facing death
the heart can generate feelings of great joy.
So, what pain cannot be turned into bliss?

Radiating Mindfulness

In this world,
I hope to radiate positivity and mindfulness.

In this universe,
what am I walking with,
living with, and
giving with?
Mindfulness.

Even as I'm walking past another person,
I never want to miss an opportunity to smile.
Using my earnest heart,
I bring warmth to myself,
to others, and
to the world.

The Law of Karma

If we enthusiastically give others
happiness and support,
continuously,
one day these gifts will return to us—
from near, far, and
even from places
we never could have imagined!
This is the power of cause and effect,
this is karma!

Infinite Lifetimes, Infinite Hope

Life is an infinite continuation—
it does not simply end in this one lifetime.
So, why not adjust our focus from the present
and gaze into the limitless future
to create even more beautiful tomorrows?

Our Inner Tug-Of-War

The greatest challenge in our aspiration to help others
is the struggle between
self-centered and other-centered.
Once we have overcome this hurdle,
cherishing others will become second nature.
When this habit becomes a part of us,
on the rare occasions
our ego arises,
we'll be flustered.
Embarrassed, we'll realize:
Is it about myself again?
This isn't the way to happiness!
So—
again
it is just a matter of habit.

The Greater Our Burdens,
The Stronger Our Bones

After training through and
overcoming difficulties time again,
you realize:
the heavier my burdens,
the stronger I become.
Until one day,
you are as strong as Atlas,
able to hold up the skies.

Even as others fall,
you stay standing,
and seeing your persistence
the people around you have the courage to
lift themselves up.
So through accumulating
more and more experience from
undergoing more and more hardship,
practitioners—
one after another—
gain the strength and resilience to stand tall.

Unveiling Enlightenment

In every conflict,
if I can self-reflect and recognize:
I am cloaked in the darkness of saṃsāra,
so
I tend to confuse suffering and happiness,
I have not yet reached enlightenment—
then
every conflict is a stepping stone,
pushing me to surpass my limitations to
reach enlightenment
so I can clearly see the profound truth
behind all things, and
extract the roots of all suffering.

Retaliating with Wisdom

When negativity arrives,
we feel pain sticking to our body and mind.
Though we struggle,
suffering stalks.
Though we fight,
suffering clings.
We must use wisdom to retaliate,
to chisel at our afflictions, and
weaken their grasp.

In the Wake of Darkness

Do not be bound by the struggles we face.
Though they are like darkness,
sullen and daunting,
they are only temporary.
When we bravely overcome them
we will find the glowing moon
hidden behind the clouds
so beautiful and so pristine.

Our heart is like the deep and boundless sky.
On the day we truly know it
we will realize
most vast is *heart*.
most beautiful is *heart*.

A Practitioner's Joy

As one fills a plate with a great spiritual feast—
rich and luxurious—
the need for material things is
pushed into the smallest recesses of the mind.

The noise of
resplendent clothing and delicious food
is replaced by
serenity,
the calm of meditation under the moonlight.

A flower beyond the mire
stands tall,
through all of life's seasons—
blooming—
its fragrance drifting
far and wide.

Facing the Fruits of Karma

In the process of learning,
if difficulties develop,
be alert!

Let's not back away.
Break through the challenge, and
that's it!
Backing away—running—does not help
because if the fruits from our past karma have ripened,
we cannot escape them.
So, let's face and resolve them for good.

Expediency

As soon as we turn our gaze toward
the question of dying,
we will recognize that
all of the other issues in life are small.
The greatest issue to consider:
death is of utmost importance—
impermanence strikes quickly.

Because we have so little time,
we must clearly decide
what is most important
and most essential
to expend our efforts on.

Freeing Ourselves

To leave suffering and attain happiness
our perspective—
adopting one rooted in wisdom—
is of utmost importance.

There are moments
we feel particularly misunderstood or hurt.
At this time
observe our thoughts and actions—
are we expecting others to pay?
Do we want to hurt them in return?
If so,
stop.
Cast away the burden of revenge.
Release ourselves from
this adverse thinking and behaviour.

Soaring Above Quicksand

Let our minds break free from our emotions' control!

Can I have a pair of wings,
to soar above the quicksand of my afflicted feelings?
And what is this pair of wings?

It is the heart that will not acquiesce to feelings.
These feelings
do not allow us to create virtuous karma,
do not allow us inner cultivation.

It is the heart that aspires to surpass its limits,
making its dreams a reality.

Transcending

The path of the practitioner is one of
transcending the self—
confronted with a challenge,
we can choose views rooted in wisdom, contemplating:
How can I break through this
accurately and wholeheartedly?
By using the wisdom I have learned
to surpass my difficulties,
I keep earning the joy of transcending myself!

Let the Heart Illuminate the World

The heart of the wise is like a light upon the world,
first teaching us
to be aware of our minds,
to understand losses and gains,
to know the causes for calamity and fortune.
Then we may alter our suffering and
the causes for suffering.
Then we may extensively plant happiness and
the causes for happiness.

If we can dive into the philosophies of the wise,
we are kindling our light.
This light will illuminate ourselves and others.
One day,
this light will illuminate the world.

Awaken

Their mistakes are like
glowing red steel
burning our heart,
a pain almost impossible to heal.
Walking away,
the heart lingers.
Staying,
it clings to what's broken
but there's nowhere left to turn.

Caught in between—
suffering—
at a glance this pain is caused by others.
But, what of the heart?
Has the heart become accustomed to pain?
Clearly,
it is shrouded in yesterday's sorrows,
habitually reliving hurts,
repeatedly self-harming.

Why not awaken?

The power to feel joy is always within us,
because joy is a skill we can cultivate and practice!
Instead of nurturing old wounds
and allowing them to grow,
nurture joy,
allow it to blossom.

Religion and World Peace

Interfaith harmony can be
a wonderful influence on world peace.
If all religions interact harmoniously,
like friends,
helping and supporting each other
with compassion,
diligently enhancing
mutual respect, admiration, and friendship,
then this spirit
will be a great catalyst for world peace.

Stepping Away from Suffering

When you are in pain
and it feels unbearable,
so much so it's difficult to breathe,
we can try relieving the pain
by thinking:

If, in this moment,
the suffering I experience
can melt away
the pain felt by all sentient beings,
this suffering can find meaning.

Thinking like this,
our suffering can become more bearable.
Why?

The suffering within saṃsāra
is known to be rooted in
a self-cherishing attachment from beginningless time.
So, if we can shift our focus onto others,
our anguish can become less salient,
and our pain can feel less painful.

Expanding Horizons

At times our vision narrows
like the fine tip of a needle.
We pointedly stare at what is before us.
A situation—
sharp
and
difficult to parry.

But once we place what is before us
into the grand scheme of our life,
or on the journey of our infinite lives,
or within the context of countless beings' lives,
or from the eyes of those who are enlightened—
then, how does the situation seem?

Braving Through Limits

When we are determined to give away
an item we really love,
what do we receive in return?
I've triumphed over myself.
I've resisted wanting to keep, store, and hoard,
insisting:
"This is mine!"

Blessed with the joy of braving through our limits,
we come to realize:

I did something amazing today. I surpassed myself!

Stepping Stones to Enlightenment

The most splendid scenery,
the most radiant light,
is our kindness,
our understanding, and
our embracing of others
from the bottom of our heart.
Therefore, it is important to learn to
resolve disagreements with others, and
to use our misunderstandings as bridges to
strengthen our bonds of friendship.
This is transforming obstacles into
stepping stones on the path to enlightenment.

The Giving Tree

Standing before an ancient tree,
we may marvel at how lush its leaves are and
how sturdy its trunk is,
and some,
with a heart of gratitude will ponder:

Years ago,
who planted this tree
so that today
I have this shade?

CHAPTER FIVE

Meditations

Meditation on Patience

Why are bothersome people like this?
Because they have difficulties.

In truth, everyone has difficulties.
There are no reasons to further add fuel
to the fires of conflict,
or to aggravate already open wounds.
Let's create safe spaces for them
to survive through trying times
as our shortcomings
are yet to be
resolved.

Meditation on Loving Words

Words.
Do they have expressions?

Words from my mouth,
words to your ears.
Then come
smiles
warmth
motivation
encouragement.

This is the power of loving words.

They transform
distress into joy,
despair into enthusiasm,
indifference into gratitude.

This is the power of loving words.

I use my genuine smile and hold your gaze,
expressing to you my sincerest gratitude.
Can your heart be filled with warmth?

May my loving words be flowers blooming in your heart,
filling the world with sweet fragrance.

Meditation for When We've Been Hurt

If your heart has been hurt by someone
and you still have to face them,
perhaps you can try something new.
Calm your mind and reflect:

In the past,
what kind intentions did that person have?
In the past,
what kind gestures did that person do?
In the past,
in how many instances and
in how many ways
did that person accompany me through life's struggles?

Meditation on Hope

Precisely because the problem stems from within,
infinite lifetimes will bring infinite hope!

Because in this present moment we can see:
Is my current thought appropriate?
Am I motivated by unsullied intentions?

Making the most of our present thought is
making the most of our future happiness.

Meditation on Compassion

If thoughts and words can create miracles,
then what of
compassionate thoughts and words?
Even more so,
they can deeply benefit all.

Compassion is
like the moon—
perfect and pure.
It can bring calm to those who are worrying
and bring serenity to this world.

Breathing with Nature

When you walk past trees,
they are telling you:
breathe deeply.

When you see flowers,
they are telling you:
breathe deeply.

Even in the sky,
each cloud breathes deeply as it sails.
The whole world is filled with whispers:
breathe deeply.

Can you hear it?

Meditation on Kindness

I am resolved to create positive karma.
No matter the circumstance,
I aspire to create karma
that will be of benefit to others.

When this becomes a habit,
we will be joyful.

Meditation: A Gift for All

When reciting the mantra
Om mani padme hum,
we can aspire to recite it for every single living being,
and when we do
it is as if every one of them is receiving our present.

So, sometimes, sitting in your own room,
you can send a gift to all sentient beings!

At that moment
the boundaries between people melt away
and the channels between our hearts open.

Meditation on Love

May we all
be good to our parents,
be kind to our friends,
be involved with our communities, and
be generous with our care.

Whether we are
on an airplane,
on a train,
on a road—
wherever we may be—
remember to love.

Isn't this a beautiful thing?

Meditation for Stress

Sometimes it feels as if all that is within and without
are in disarray—
anxiety and stress drown us.

What can we do?
Breathe deeply.
Again,
breathe deeply.

Shift your focus.
Concentrate on inhale and on exhale.
As the breath slowly steadies and
anxiety and stress slowly diminish,
the heart will follow suit,
calming.

Let us practice this.

Meditation on Tuning Inwards

Every time we tune inwards
our efforts are not wasted.
In time,
our heart will no longer be
as bound and hurt by suffering.

When time and time again we tune our attention—
turning it away from the outside
and bringing it inwards
paying attention to our body, speech, and mind,
paying attention to our breath—
we will discover things we normally do not notice, and
avoid some of our ongoing problems and pains.

Let the heart—
time and again—
return to calm
return to gentleness
return to forgiveness and compassion.
When we become adept in this training,
the freedom in our lives
endlessly increases.

A Meditation on Virtuous Friends

Regardless of how much hardship we encounter,
or how much loneliness we may feel,
from young to old,

may we be surrounded by many virtuous friends
who can share our burdens,
who can offer us support—
and may we all live a life filled with beauty.

Meditation for a Changing World

At certain moments in time,
a heart radiates with a sincere wish:
May all living beings have happiness and
the causes for happiness.
This can genuinely affect the world.

A Meditation on Communication

When communicating,
hold the desire
to understand others' challenges while listening.
Find ways to create avenues
for them to express themselves.

With proactive thoughts using
equality, respect, amiability, and altruism
let's build a ladder of communication.
Slowly and steadily,
have a conversation.
Slowly and steadily,
learn.

Rung by rung,
we communicate.
Rung by rung,
we learn.

Bear witness to how
through communication
we grow.

Meditation Within Life's Lows

When something bad happens,
let's use the time and energy
we may spend complaining
to actively think of solutions!

Perhaps, we could consider:

What problem am I facing?
How can it be changed, and when?
What resources might be helpful?
Do I really want to change for the better?

With a proactive mindset
that actively strives to minimize our losses,
we'll grow!

In time,
we'll no longer be afraid of challenges
because when we encounter life's lows,
we'll learn to harvest more courage and wisdom.
Perhaps they'll even inspire us to
find great mentors and make great friends—
perhaps they'll even inspire a more exuberant life.

Meditation on Accepting Criticism

Sometimes
those who care about us will give us some suggestions.
Perhaps
hearing them brings us some discomfort
but
as long as we maintain
an open mind and an attitude willing to learn
we will be able to feel others' thoughtful intentions
and create many friendships.
We will not close our doors.

Having people with the courage to point things out to us,
whether we are conscious of these things or not,
let us first accept their words
and observe their suggestions.
An extra pair of eyes looking out for us
is also welcome company.

Meditation to Harvest Serenity

I was actually nervous
struggling
jumbling my thoughts
and finally—
I see what
I am doing.

Sitting under a tree
observing our mind
the heart's
perturbed flights,
the mind's
uncontrolled thoughts
quieten,
like birds
calmly nestled in the grass.
At this time
we can harvest serenity.

Meditation on Tea

When drinking tea,
see the leaves
slowly drifting down.
Leaf after leaf
drifting down.
All of the leaves,
lying on the bottom of the cup.

Allowing frustration to settle,
time and again,
our heart
surrenders to gentle waves
bedewed and sweet—
savouring life's sweet aftertaste.

The Beauty Around Us

Gaze—
upon a blade of grass,
its colours enter our mind.

Gaze—
upon a drop of dew,
its lucidity glistens in our heart.

From a drop of dew,
serenity enters our world,
luminous,
shining through.

Many things in our lives—
                    gazing at a blade of grass,
                    gazing at a bead of dew,
can bring joy, meaning, and gratitude.

In those moments,
our heart becomes boundless,
experiencing the world's beauty.

Meditation for All Beings

May all beings respect and care for one another.
May all beings cherish the world that we have
and the resources that we share.

We love the blue skies,
we love the green earth,
we love the lush forests,
we love the clear waters.

Let us show our love
through
action.

Meditation on Harmony

May all the birds soaring in the skies
may all the fish swimming in the waters
may all the critters shuffling in the grasses
feel this prayer for harmony and reciprocity.

May this wish permeate the universe
so all sentient beings can feel
comfort and warmth
within the depths of their hearts.

Toolkit for a Closer Read

We aimed to make the passages widely accessible, peppered with a few Buddhist terminologies. Here are some explanations as you traverse through the book.

Afflictions: Identified as the root of our sufferings, afflictions are mental factors that disrupt our peace of mind. For a Buddhist practitioner, the true enemy to be vanquished—our own afflictions—is not external, but internal. In the Buddhist framework, there are eighty-four-thousand mental afflictions, including pride, jealousy, and anger. The three core afflictions are attachment (clinging to what we like and desiring it), hostility (rejecting what we dislike and wanting to cause harm), and ignorance (a misperception of reality, and the root of all afflictions and suffering).

Bodhisattva: Someone who has resolved to attain enlightenment in order to relieve the suffering of all sentient beings, devoting themselves entirely to the well-being of others.

Enlightenment: In Mahāyāna Buddhism, enlightenment is a state of mind free from afflictions and suffering, with all-encompassing wisdom and compassion. In Buddhism, it is believed that we can seize control of our lives and turn the tables on what is widely accepted to be constant, inevitable, and unchangeable—suffering in saṃsāra—into the state of enlightenment. Buddhism believes that every being can attain enlightenment because the mind itself is never alienated from its potential to reach enlightenment.

Good/bad: *See "virtue/non-virtue."*

Ignorance: *See "afflictions."*

Inner cultivation: The mental training to control and tame the mind. Every experience—good, bad, happiness, suffering—is determined by our own thoughts. Through contemplation and skill, all afflictions can be removed. This makes us free and empowered to shape ourselves and our future. Recognizing that the mind is never constant and has limitless potential, we have the ability to transcend all suffering. Through learning, we can deliberately choose thoughts conducive to happiness and challenge thoughts that lead to suffering. Just as athletes train in strength, musicians in dexterity, so the practitioner trains the mind. The enemy is our own afflictions. The battlefield is our own mind. The training grounds are the everyday situations we encounter.

Karma: Literally meaning "action" in Sanskrit, karma are actions of the body, speech, and mind. Within western vernacular, karma has taken shape as a fighter of justice or vengeful god. Within Buddhism, karma is much less preoccupied with punishment. It is simply an observation of a natural phenomenon, not unlike any of Newton's laws of motion, in that everything we experience—without and within—has its causes and effects. Virtuous actions (i.e., virtuous karma) lead to future experiences of happiness; non-virtuous actions (i.e., non-virtuous karma) lead to future experiences of suffering.

Leaving suffering, attaining happiness: The natural instinct of all sentient beings to want to be happy and to not suffer. In

Buddhism, we believe every action of the body, speech, and mind reflects this innate drive. Within Buddhism, the true happiness that we want to cultivate is enduring. It arises from deep contentment and inner peace and is a state free from all suffering. The key to happiness lies in our own minds.

Merit: Provisions that sustain a practitioner on the path to enlightenment. Engaging in virtuous behaviour results in merit earned. Merit can be carried with us from this lifetime to the next.

Om mani padme hum: Mantra of compassion. In Buddhism, *Om* represents the dichotomy of pure and impure within our minds. *Mani* and *padme* are the means to transform the impure to pure. *Mani*—meaning "jewel"—represents compassion; *padme*—meaning "lotus flower"—represents wisdom. *Hum* means "to combine" such that compassion and wisdom are the wings that allow us to soar from our current state to the pure state of enlightenment.

Observe Merits and Appreciate Kindness (OMAK): A contemplative practice developed by Master Jih-Chang to garner hope and strength in all situations, even amidst adversities. Rooted in Buddhist teachings, OMAK helps change our perspective and can be divided into two components. "Observe Merits" guides us to find the good qualities of a situation or person. "Appreciate Kindness" guides us to recall the benefits we receive from a situation or person, inspiring feelings of gratitude.

Repentance: In Buddhism, repentance is open acknowledgment of past behaviour. By addressing our actions and thoughts, we become conscious of our behaviour patterns and tendencies. Only then can changes be possible.

Right mindfulness: A mental factor that prevents the mind from being distracted (in Buddhist practice, right mindfulness is specifically focused on something virtuous). Right mindfulness works in tandem with vigilance—a mental factor that monitors whether the mind has wandered or is wandering—to keep our minds in focus. In this book, "right mindfulness" is used interchangeably with "mindfulness."

Saṃsāra: The cycle of rebirth that is brought about by afflictions and karma.

Self-cherishing attachment: A tendency to cling to the "'self," placing the "self" at a much higher importance than others. In Buddhism, the self-cherishing attachment is the true cause of our suffering. As such, Buddhism strives to remove the self-cherishing attachment from our minds by training our minds to shift our focus and interest onto others. Cherishing others over the self is not self-sacrificial or masochistic; rather, it is the wisest way to act in self-interest. In this book, "self-cherishing attachment" is used interchangeably with "self-centered."

Suffering: An aversive word, yet so much a part of our lives. By recognizing suffering, we can transform it. In Buddhism, suffering—comprehensive of any experience of unpleasantness, discomfort, or dissatisfaction—is a consequence of our actions, conceived by our thoughts. Within saṃsāra, suffering is a constant undercurrent born from ignorance—not seeing things as they truly are.

Virtue/non-virtue: Actions of the body, speech, and mind that lead to our experiences of happiness/unhappiness. Within Buddhism, an act is not considered virtuous or non-virtuous based on indoctrinated principle, but whether it leads to happiness *(see "leaving suffering, attaining happiness").* In this book, "virtue" is used interchangeably with "good," "positive," "healthy." The opposite is non-virtue—actions of the body, speech, and mind that lead to our personal experiences of suffering. In this book, "non-virtue" is sometimes used interchangeably with "bad," "negative," "unhealthy."

Wisdom of emptiness: A realization of the true nature of all living beings and phenomena—all are empty of intrinsic nature. Within Mahāyāna Buddhism, the wisdom of emptiness must be coupled with great compassion to reach enlightenment.

Acknowledgements

There's a key concept in Buddhism called "interdependence." It suggests everything is interconnected and nothing exists in isolation. It also wonderfully summarizes the culmination of this project after over six years. Page by page, through the collective efforts of many, the book you now hold in your hands came to life.

Our team ranged from hedge-fund analysts and scientists to those who joined the monastery fresh out of university. Despite the diversity, we are all monastic and lay students of the late Master Jih-Chang and his student, Teacher Zhen-Ru. This project was sparked by two books written in Chinese containing daily passages, excerpted from Teacher Zhen-Ru's spiritual teachings. They contain a surprising revelation: happiness is nothing short of how we shape our thoughts. Inspired by Teacher Zhen-Ru's wish to accompany everyone through life's challenges, we wanted to share these treasures with English readers. Thank you to our spiritual teachers, who used their words to guide and accompany us in our practice.

But, how to present Buddhism, with its storied 2,500-year-old wisdom, in an approachable manner to the modern western audience without losing its intent, depth, and beauty? Our first translation meeting was two hours… and we were still trudging through the first seven lines. Every word elicited hours of debate between staying true to the original text and creative delivery. We had hoped to finish the first 365 passages within one year. Before we knew it, PEI's purple lupins came and went, the white snow piled up and melted away. And we were nowhere near our goal.

Recognizing that we needed help, we reached out to our friend Kacy Lin in Toronto, who not only had a flair for English writing and rhetoric, but also is completely at home in the western culture. Thank you Kacy for joining as a full-time translator, crafting the passages with such ease and artistry, channeling Teacher Zhen-Ru's hope and strength. Within three months, Kacy had completed the first draft, and with indescribable patience sat through three-hour meetings, three to five times a week. Strict adherence to the original text and relatability to the everyday English reader continued their tug-of-war.

Reapproaching this dilemma, we found that the slow progress did not lie in writing skills, time management, or having too many cooks in the kitchen. Learning from the passages, we asked ourselves: When everything external seems to be going awry, what can I change within myself? Refocusing our internal dialogue, our conversations shifted from defending our own standpoints to listening to others. Against the canvas of PEI's blue skies and waving wildflowers, we gradually grew as a team, and as individuals.

To be honest, we were uncertain whether the final complete manuscript would ever see the light of day outside our translation team. But upon sharing a few passages with neighbours and friends on the Island, they commented on how the passages were thought-provoking. Some even asked if they could purchase copies for themselves or loved ones who were going through difficult times. To everyone out there who gave us this last push, thank you—it was key to putting this publication process in motion.

We are so fortunate to have Mo Duffy as our editorial director, Genevieve Loughlin as our publishing director, and their entire team at Pownal Street Press for their expertise. When we first told them how long it took us to finish the translation, their eyes lit up, paired with the heartiest laughter. We immediately felt the deep understanding and appreciation they had for our efforts. Our sincerest gratitude to Mo, for your infectious enthusiasm and never-ending creativity. And Gen, for your vision of this book and excellent time-management skills. Without the two of you, we might have taken another six years, at least. Thank you for accepting our team dynamics and believing in us. We'd also like to thank Emma Campanaro, for sharing your insights on our manuscript; Alison Strumberger, for putting on the finishing polish to this manuscript with your thoughtful and meticulous edits; Jordan Beaulieu, for designing each page to fit the specific tones of this book; and Ashley Macdonald, for introducing the book to distributors and bringing these passages into the hands of readers.

We are privileged to collaborate with our illustrator, Clara Encinas, whose intricate and delicate artwork not only captured our hearts, but also reflected a gentleness and clarity that we envisioned for this book. We believe that Clara's elegant artwork is simply a manifestation of the quiet grace in her heart. Thank you for your patience and trust in us, all the way from Spain.

Lastly, to you, the reader. Thank you for letting us be a part of your journey. We are honoured to bring this 5,000–hour labour of love into your hands.

About the Authors

Zhen-Ru

Zhen-Ru, affectionately called Teacher by her students, was born in Heilongjiang province, China. As a child, Zhen-Ru felt inexplicable sorrow regarding the widely accepted phenomenon of parting with loved ones in life and death. As she grew older, she became increasingly contemplative about death, a seemingly unexplainable and inevitable tragedy that would befall all. So, armed with the simple question "why?" she began her humble—yet unwavering—pursuit for an answer. Searching far and wide—scouring books, consulting doctors, and questioning scholars—she eventually found an answer in Buddhism.

Traversing mountains in search of a spiritual teacher, she became a disciple of eminent Tibetan Buddhist masters, Honourable Harwa Jamyang Lochu Rinpoche, as well as Labrang Monastery's illustrious teachers Master Gendun Gyatso (1932-2007) and Master Lobsang Gyatso (1946-2009). Later, she encountered Master Jih-Chang (1929-2004), a respected monk from Taiwan who dedicated his entire life to teaching and spreading awareness of *The Great Treatise on the Stages of the Path to Enlightenment (Lam Rim Chen Mo),* a fundamental Tibetan Buddhist text on enlightenment composed in the 15th century by renowned teacher, Je Tsongkhapa. After years of studying with him, Zhen-Ru became Master Jih-Chang's principal disciple. Eventually, Master Jih-Chang would entrust her with the role of spiritual teacher to guide his monastic and lay students in their study and practice of Buddhism.

When Zhen-Ru shares her insights on Buddhism, her words flow freely like a stream of clear water down a mountain valley. When she touches on the complexities hidden within the heart, people find within her words empowerment, and the strength to bring greater gratitude, love, and compassion into their everyday lives.

Though she is revered as a spiritual teacher, Zhen-Ru believes her true place is as a student—an eternal practitioner, forever seeking refuge in the Buddha.

She hopes, in this daunting world, that we find peace, compassion, forgiveness, and love, not only by searching for them in other things, but by turning toward introspection, and reflecting on the heart.

At a time when fear, instability, and powerlessness seem to infiltrate our every moment, with gentleness she hopes to remind us:

"My dear, let us not despair."

Amrita Translation Foundation

With virtue as a guiding light, Amrita Translation Foundation is committed to striving for a brighter tomorrow. Its mission is to preserve and make Buddhism more accessible through translation of teachings as well as collection of Buddhist artefacts. To ensure the essence of Buddhism is passed down to future generations, Amrita's team of monastic translators has dedicated their lives to the study and practice of Buddhist teachings. They are educated and trained in the rigorous Five Great Treatises curriculum, with roots tracing to the Tibetan and Nalanda traditions.

The team spent over six years translating Zhen-Ru's passages—sound bites based on Buddhist teachings—hoping to preserve the essence and convey the everyday applicability.

Kacy Lin

Kacy Lin is a translator who specializes in the translation of Buddhist works from Mandarin to English. She holds a master's degree in psycho-spiritual studies from the University of Toronto, as well as a bachelor's in English literature (with minors in Buddhism and visual arts). She has dedicated many years to the translation and practice of Buddhist teachings.

Kacy's deep understanding of both Buddhist philosophy and western spirituality has enabled her to render complex teachings with clarity and precision. In her translations, she focuses on both the practical elements of Buddhism and the beauty of Teacher Zhen-Ru's passages.

Being in this world,

this is the most beautiful thing,

encouraging ourselves and others

to become more kind and more compassionate

is like carrying a bright light,

forever spreading *hope*